JOE BONAMASSA • DUST BOWL

CONTENTS

Transcribed by Jeff Jacobson and Paul Pappas

Cherry Lane Music Company
Director of Publications/Project Editor: Mark Phillips

ISBN 978-1-60378-397-2

Copyright © 2012 Cherry Lane Music Company
International Copyright Secured
All Rights Reserved

The music, text, design and graphics in this publication are protected by copyright law. Any duplication or transmission,
by any means, electronic, mechanical, photocopying, recording or otherwise, is an infringement of copyright.

Visit our website at www.cherrylaneprint.com

DUST BOWL

As Joe Bonamassa grows his reputation as one of the world's greatest guitar players, he is also evolving into a charismatic blues-rock star and singer-songwriter of stylistic depth and emotional resonance. His ability to connect with live concert audiences is transformational, and his new album, *Dust Bowl,* brings that energy to his recorded music more powerfully than ever before. *Dust Bowl* is Bonamassa's ninth studio release on his own J&R Adventures label, which he created with his entrepreneurial partner and longtime manager, Roy Weisman. It was produced by Kevin "Caveman" Shirley (Black Crowes, Aerosmith, Led Zeppelin), making it their sixth collaboration in five years. Shirley most recently produced Bonamassa's 2010 release, *Black Rock,* along with the 2010 debut album from Black Country Communion, Bonamassa's English-American rock band with Glenn Hughes (Deep Purple), Jason Bonham (Led Zeppelin, Foreigner) and Derek Sherinian (Dream Theater, Billy Idol) and its follow-up, BCC's sophomore album simply titled *2,* released June 2011.

Dust Bowl debuted at #1 on the *Billboard* Blues Chart and #37 on *Billboard*'s Top 200 Chart—making it Bonamassa's highest-selling and chart-ranking US debut to date—and quickly received an abundance of glowing critical acclaim. *Premier Guitar* called it "A blues-rock achievement...his best record to date," and gave it 4.5 out of 5 stars. *The Dallas Morning News* described it as "thematic and expansive...a blues-rocking tour de force from an artist who knows no other way of making music." *USA Today* said, "What sets this album apart is the superior songwriting and the ability to seamlessly inject sounds from other genres into the mix." And *The Orange County Register* said Joe is "unquestionably among our greatest living guitarists, destined to be counted among the greatest of all time."

Dust Bowl was recorded in sessions at Black Rock Studios in Santorini, Greece, Ben's Studio in Nashville, TN, The Cave in Malibu, CA, and The Village in Los Angeles, CA. It combines the gritty, blues-based tones of Bonamassa's first albums with the fluid, genre-defying sounds he's mastered in the years since, and adds a dash of country from Joe's collaborations with the best of Nashville, including legends Vince Gill and John Hiatt. *"Dust Bowl,"* Shirley explains, "is very firmly rooted in the blues, but definitely explores the outer reaches of the genre and showcases Joe's amazing virtuosity as he digs deep into his psyche in some lengthy and blistering guitar solos."

Photo by Christie Goodwin

In addition to the Bonamassa originals, the album features songs like the John Hiatt/ John Porter–penned "Tennessee Plates," on which Hiatt duets with Bonamassa and Vince Gill lends his signature guitar stylings. Gill also plays on "Sweet Rowena," a song he composed with frequent writing partner Pete Wasner. Arlan Scheirbaum, Beth Hart, and Blondie Chaplin play on the Michael Kamen/Tim Curry track "No Love on the Street," and Glenn Hughes sings on the Paul Rodgers–penned "Heartbreaker."

Bonamassa circles the globe playing an average of 200 shows a year, and his mind-blowing guitar wizardry and electrifying stage presence are selling out progressively larger venues all the time. Ben Wener from *The Orange County Register* said, "I haven't seen anything so dazzling since Steve Ray Vaughan at the Wiltern in '86." *The Columbus Dispatch* hailed a recent show as "a night of wailing, energy-drenched solos that never ceased to impress," while the *Reading Eagle* called it a "tour de force performance steeped in blues." *The Grand Rapids Press* said Joe is "in a league of his own as the best blues man of his era."

Ongoing journeyman touring is a given, and looking beyond *Dust Bowl,* Bonamassa will continue his recording collaboration with producer Kevin Shirley, who says, "It's great working with Joe and seeing him enjoy the discovery of all these places he can go. He's an artist who can play anything; there are so many facets to him." Bonamassa adds, "Kevin comes up with fantastic ideas outside the box. He appreciates the blues, but pushes me, the only person besides Tom Dowd who's done that."

For more information, log on to: www.jbonamassa.com.

SLOW TRAIN

Words and Music by
Joe Bonamassa and Kevin Shirley

Gtr. 1: Capo II
Gtr. 2: Open E minor tuning, capo II:
(low to high) E-B-E-G-B-E

Intro
Very slowly ♩ = 24

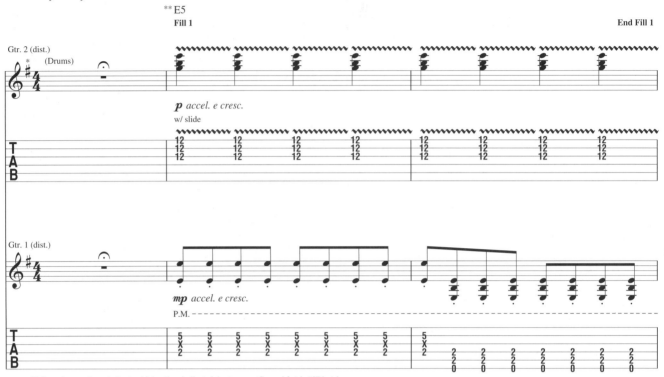

*All music sounds a whole step higher than indicated due to capo. Capoed fret is "0" in tab.
**Chord symbols reflect basic harmony.

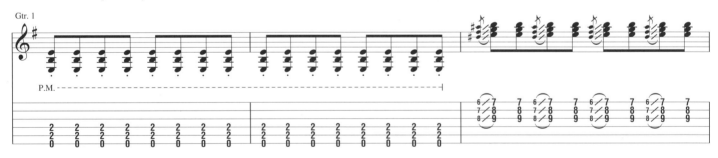

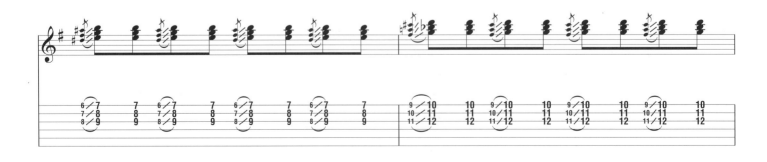

Copyright © 2011 Smokin' Joe Analog Music Co. (ASCAP) and Caveman Entertainment & Music (BMI)
International Copyright Secured   All Rights Reserved

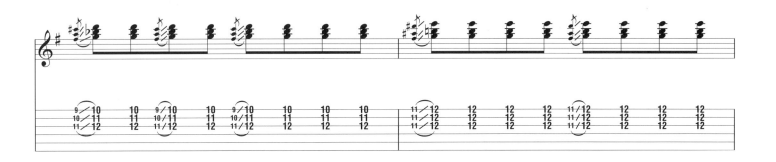

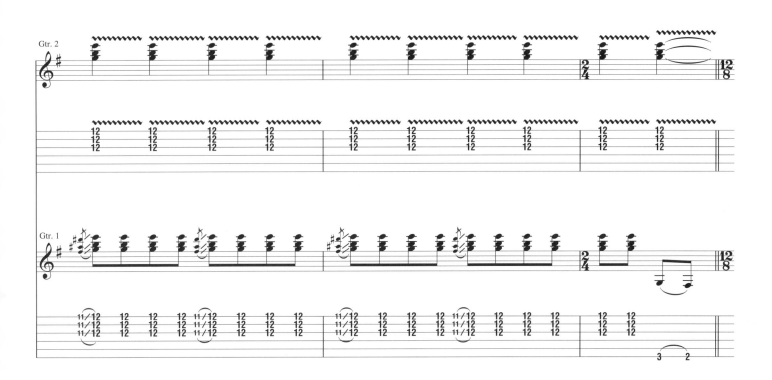

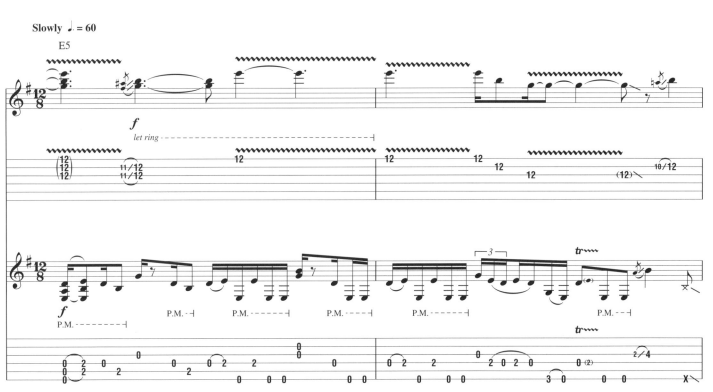

1. There's a

Verse

Gtr. 2 tacet

E5

slow train com-in', mov-in' on down the line.____

Gtr. 1

Steel wheels on i-ron rails,____ to-night I'm____ fix-in' to die.____ Woo, I

E5

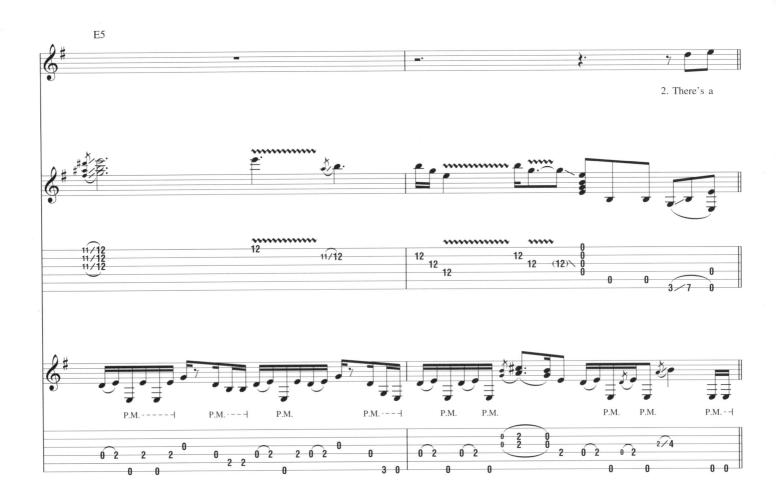

2. There's a

Verse

E5

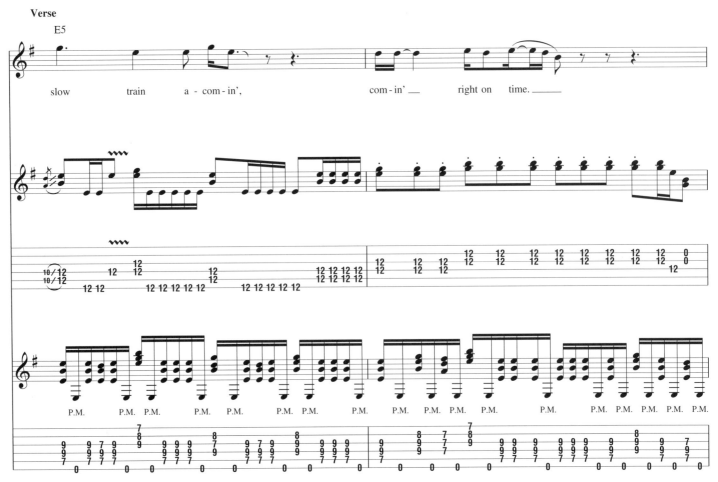

slow   train   a - com - in',   com - in' ___ right on time. ___

8

Smoke-stacks and bot-tled light-ning, this jump-er on the line. Woo, I can't

Gtr. 2 tacet
A5

do with-out it an-y-more, pret-ty ma-ma. Yes, I can't do with-out it an-y-more.

Gtr. 1

E5

'Cause when the

Gtr. 2

w/ pick & middle finger

Gtr. 1

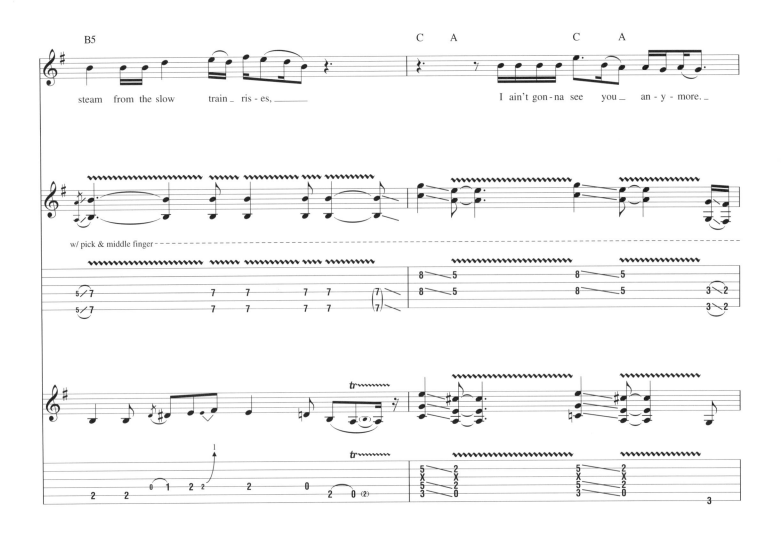

steam   from   the   slow   train _ ris - es, _____   I   ain't   gon - na   see   you _   an - y - more. _

11

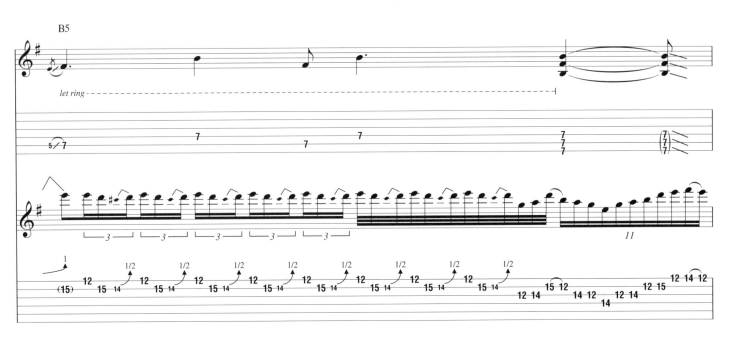

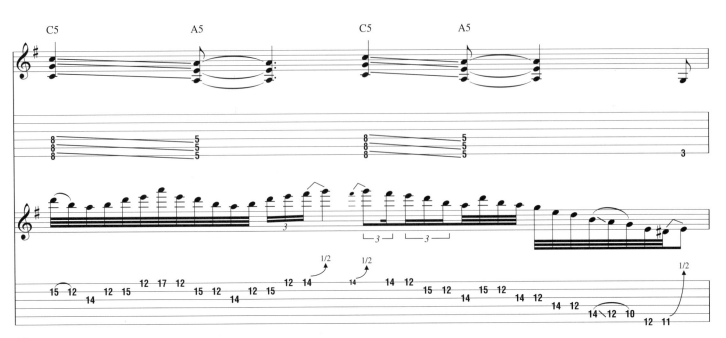

3. There's a

Verse

Gtr. 2 tacet

E5

slow train a-com-in' to march us home from war. ____ With my

leath-er ____ boots and my hav-er-sack, ____ sure can't_ take it no more. ____ Woo, I

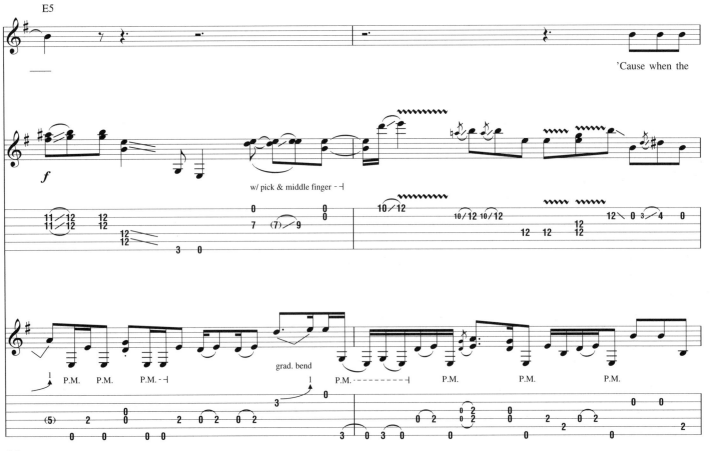

steam   from the slow   train ris - es, _____   I'm gon-na cry   for you   just __ the same. _

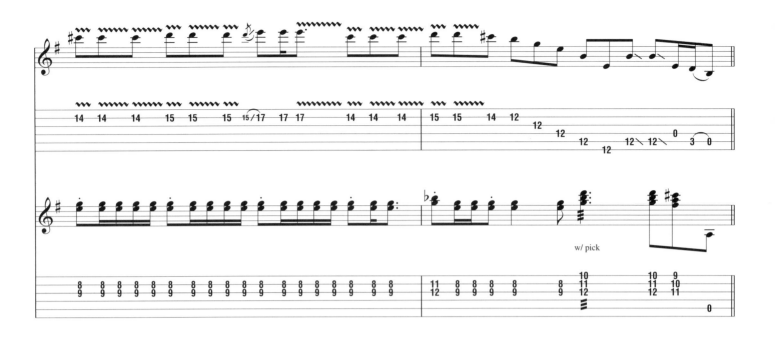

Guitar Solo

E5

4. Well, there's a

Verse
Gtr. 2 tacet
E5

slow __ train com-in', __ car-ry-ing the might-y work-er hordes. __

Gtr. 1

mp

Eight-een __ days in the cot-ton field, e-nough to put a man out of *coup __ d'a-mour.* Woo, it's

Gtr. 2

Gtr. 1

f

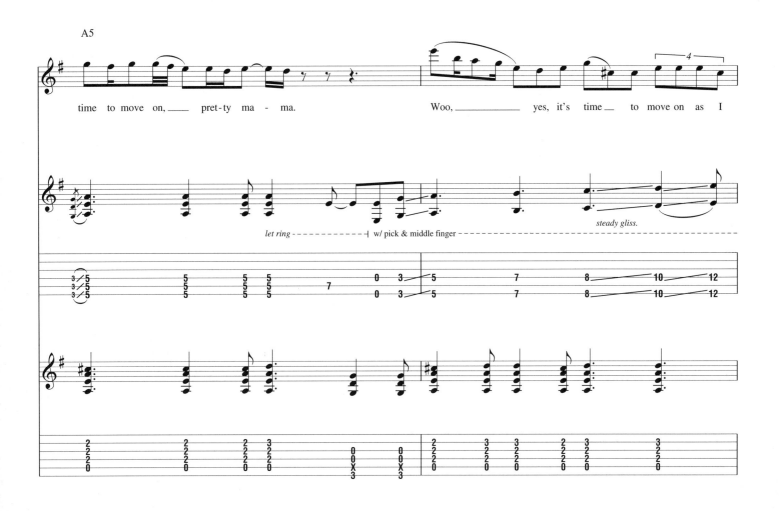

time to move on, ___ pret-ty ma - ma.   Woo, _____ yes, it's time __ to move on as I

go. ___   As the

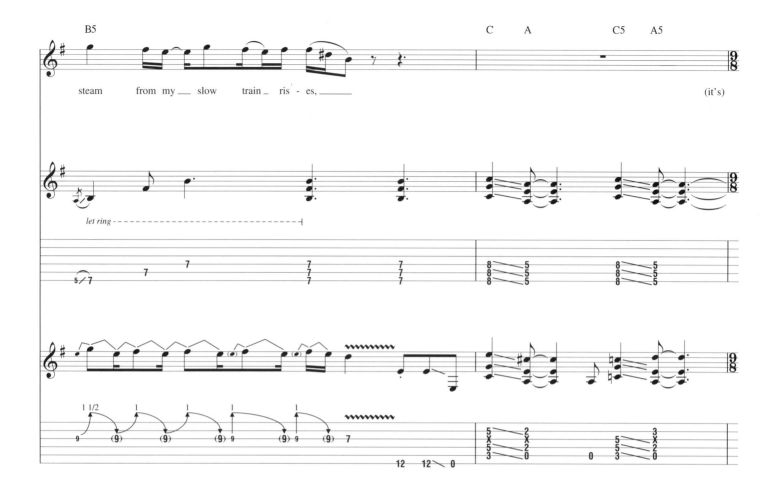

steam   from my ___ slow   train ___ ris - es, ___   (it's)

Free time

time   for   me   to   get   on   -   board. ___

A tempo

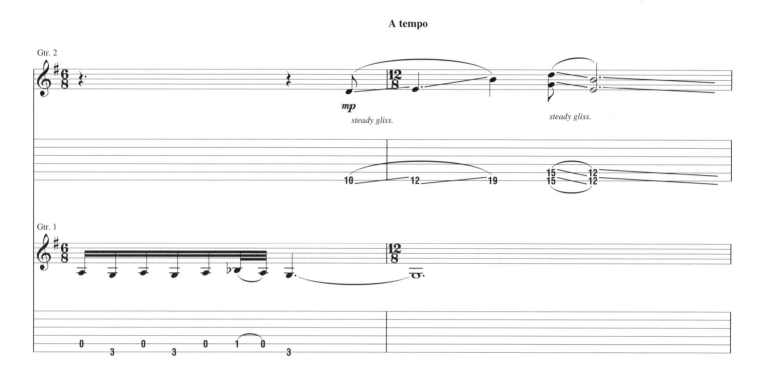

Free time

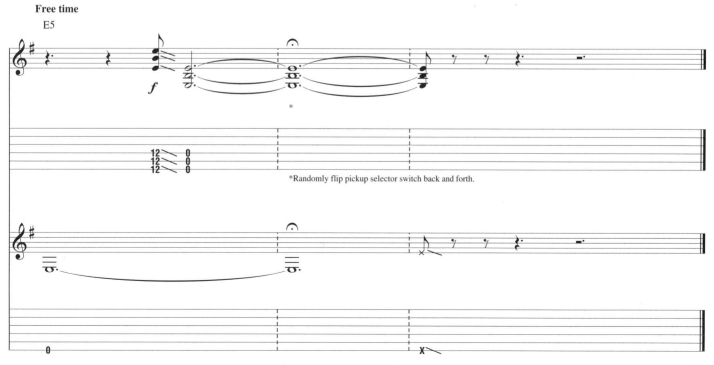

*Randomly flip pickup selector switch back and forth.

DUST BOWL

Words and Music by
Joe Bonamassa

Gtr. 6: Open Em tuning, capo 4th fret:
(low to high) E-B-E-G-B-E

Intro

Moderately slow ♩ = 92

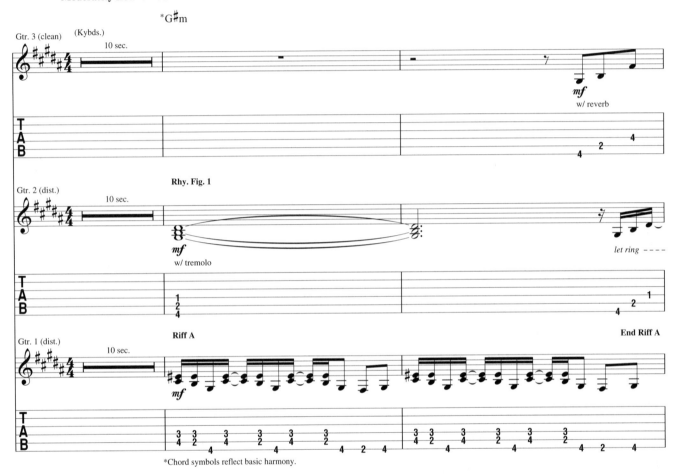

*Chord symbols reflect basic harmony.

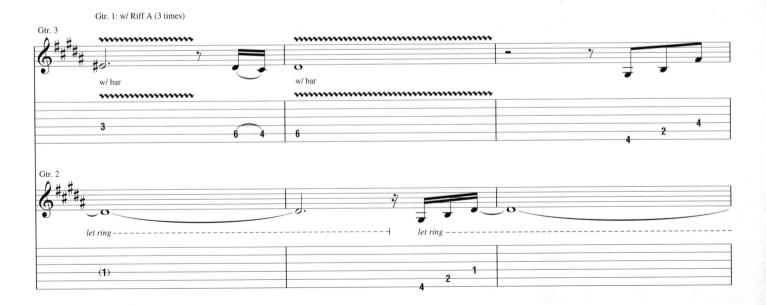

Copyright © 2011 Smokin' Joe Analog Music Co. (ASCAP)
International Copyright Secured All Rights Reserved

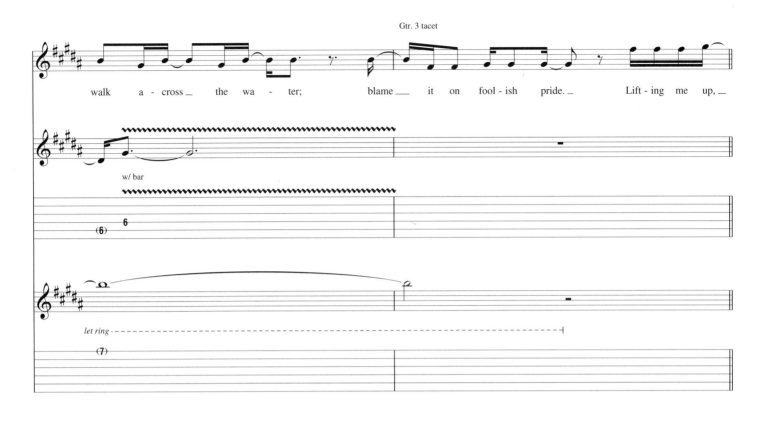

walk a-cross__ the wa-ter; blame__ it on fool-ish pride.__ Lift-ing me up,__

w/ bar

let ring -

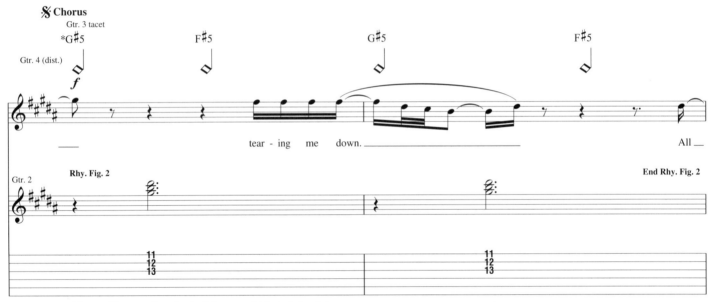

𝄋 Chorus

Gtr. 3 tacet

*G#5   F#5   G#5   F#5

Gtr. 4 (dist.)

f

tear - ing me down._____ All __

Gtr. 2   Rhy. Fig. 2   End Rhy. Fig. 2

*See top of first page of song for chord diagrams pertaining to rhythm slashes.

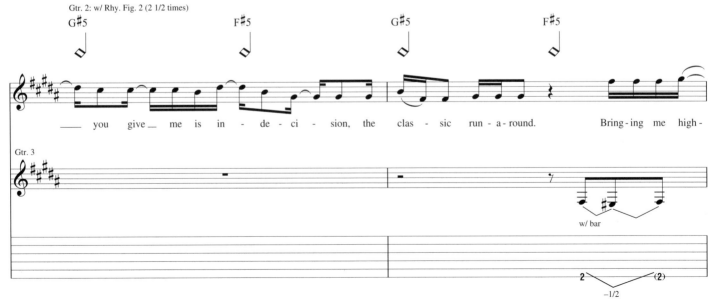

Gtr. 2: w/ Rhy. Fig. 2 (2 1/2 times)

G#5   F#5   G#5   F#5

__ you give__ me is in - de - ci - sion, the clas - sic run - a - round. Bring-ing me high-

Gtr. 3

w/ bar

Gtr. 1: w/ Riff B

2. Dia - monds and

Verse

Gtr. 1: w/ Riff B (4 times)
Gtr. 3 tacet

pearls, ___   you're that   kind of   girl. ___   You

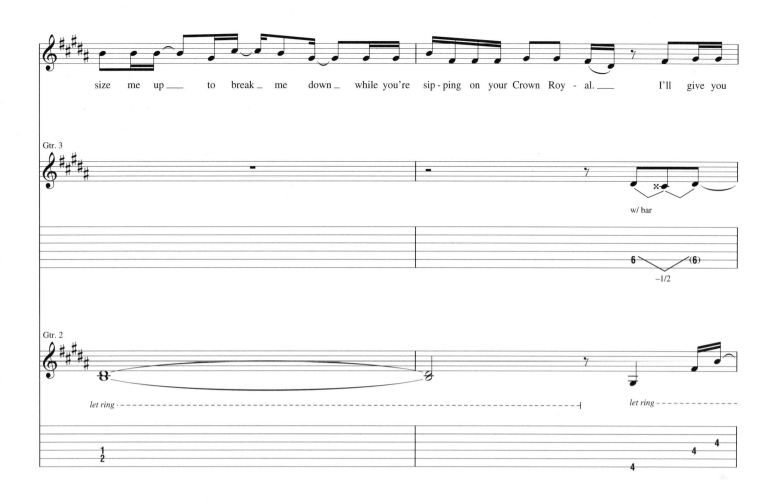

size me up ___ to break __ me down ___ while you're sip - ping on your Crown Roy - al. ___ I'll give you

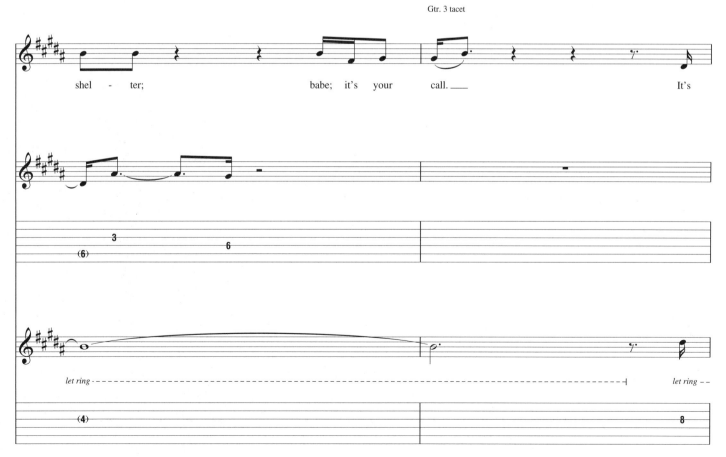

shel - ter; babe; it's your call. ___ It's

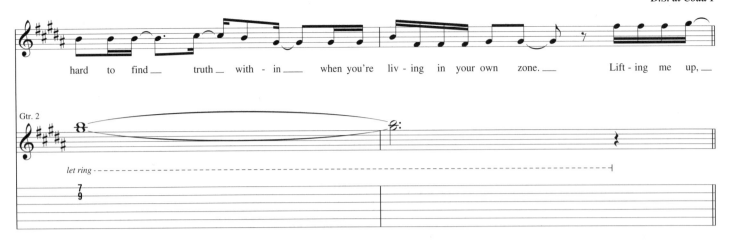

hard to find ___ truth ___ with - in ___ when you're liv - ing in your own zone. ___ Lift - ing me up,

⊕ Coda 1

Interlude

Gtr. 4 tacet
*Gtr. 5: w/ Riff B (2 times)

Gtr. 3 tacet

- ing in a dust bowl. ___

*Gtr. 5 (clean) played **p**.

Pitch: D
**Pick behind nut.

Guitar Solo

Gtr. 1: w/ Riff B (4 times)
Gtr. 2: w/ Rhy. Fig. 1 (2 times)

***Symbol in parentheses represents chord name respective to capoed guitar.
Symbol above reflects actual sounding chord. Capoed fret is "0" in tab.
Gtr. 6 sounds a major 3rd higher than indicated due to capo.

28

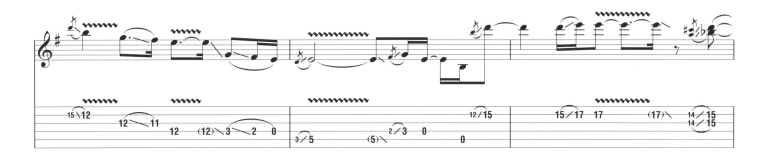

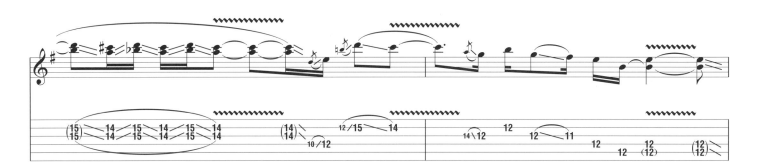

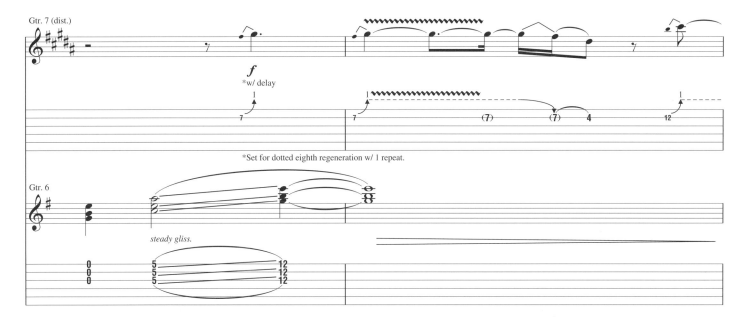

*Set for dotted eighth regeneration w/ 1 repeat.

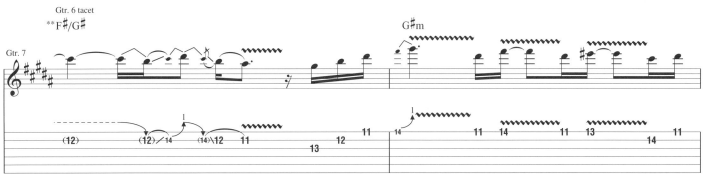

**Chords played by kybds. (next 7 meas.).

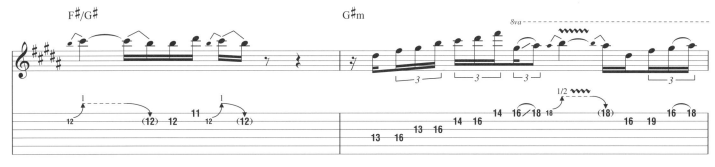

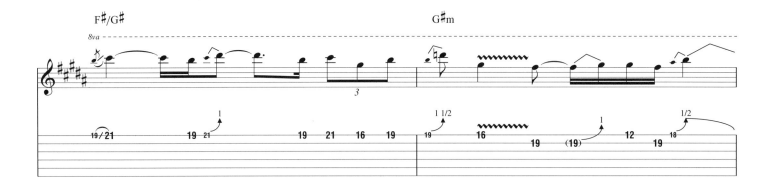

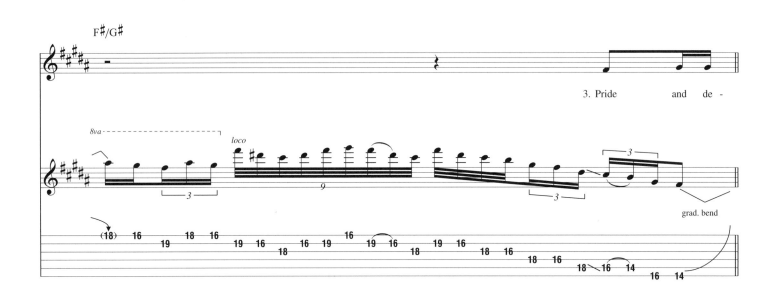

Verse

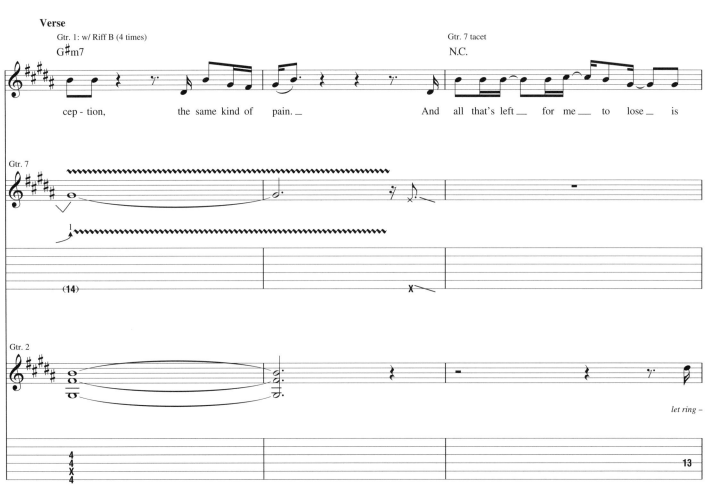

meant _ for you to gain. _ Play - ing it close, _ steal - ing your time. _ But

D.S. al Coda 2

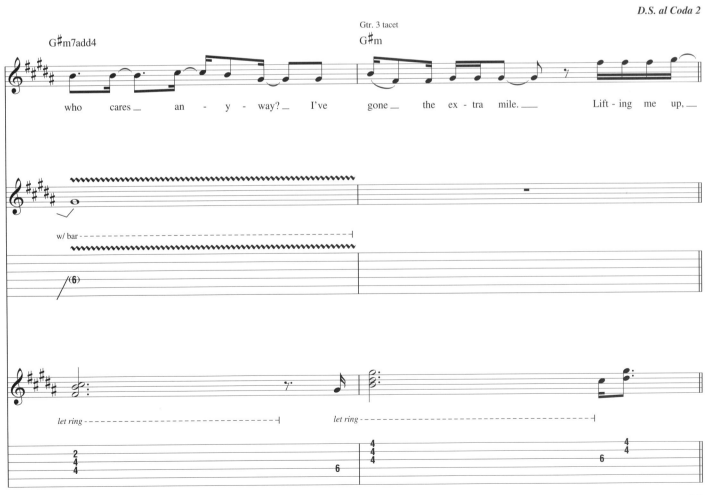

who cares _ an - y - way? _ I've gone _ the ex - tra mile. _ Lift - ing me up, _

Coda 2

Outro

Gtr. 4 tacet

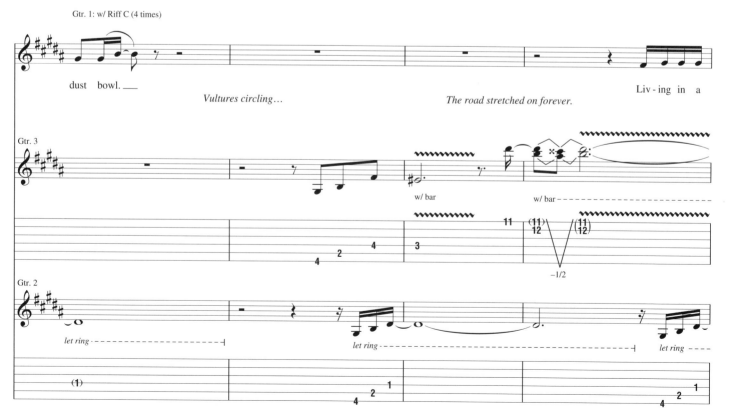

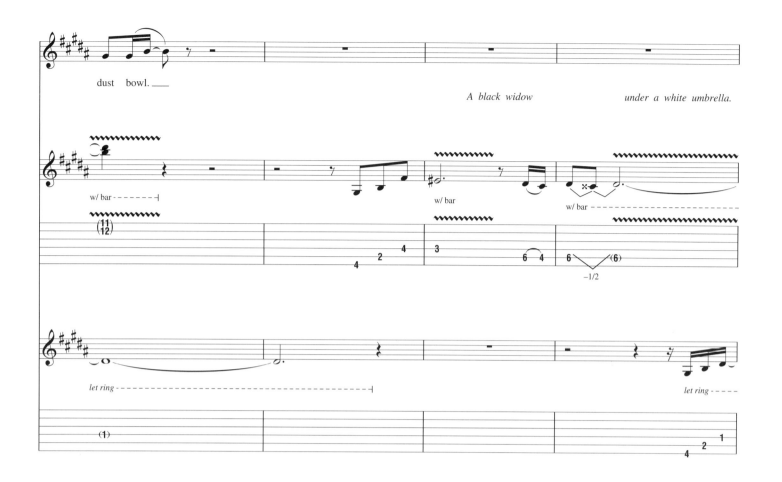

dust bowl. ____

A black widow   *under a white umbrella.*

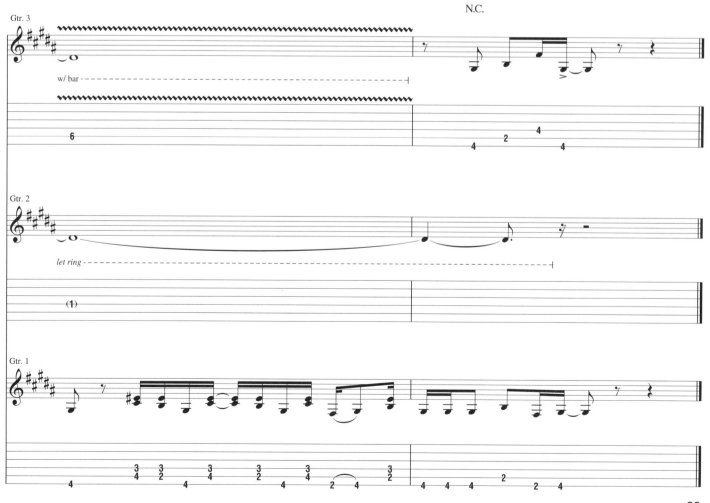

33

TENNESSEE PLATES

Words and Music by
John Hiatt and Mike Porter

Intro
Moderately fast ♩ = 152

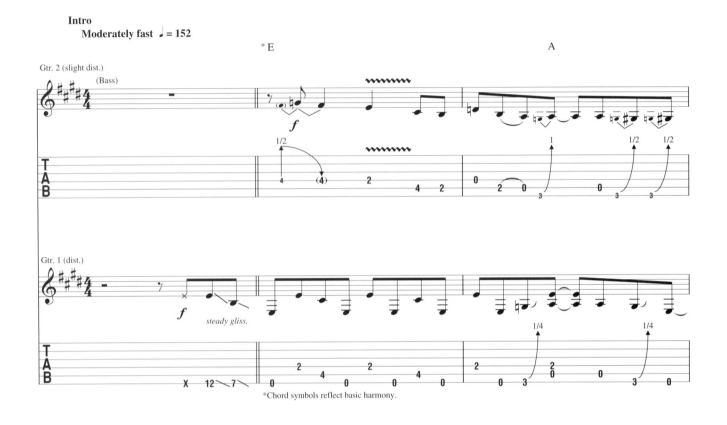

*Chord symbols reflect basic harmony.

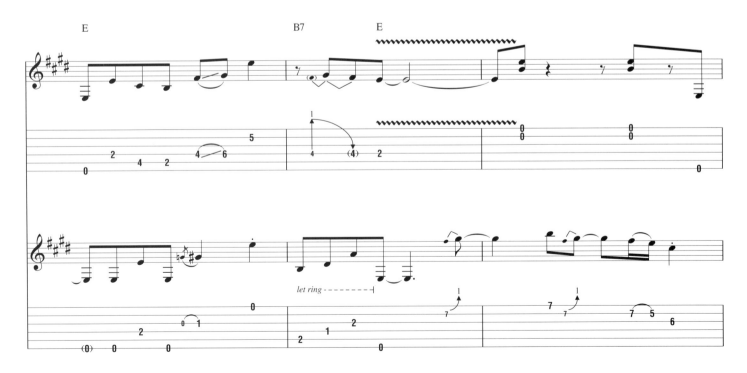

34

Copyright © 1988 by Universal Music - Careers and Brother Gekko Music
International Copyright Secured   All Rights Reserved

Verse

woke up in a ho - tel, ___ did - n't know what to do. I turned the T - V on, ___ wrote a

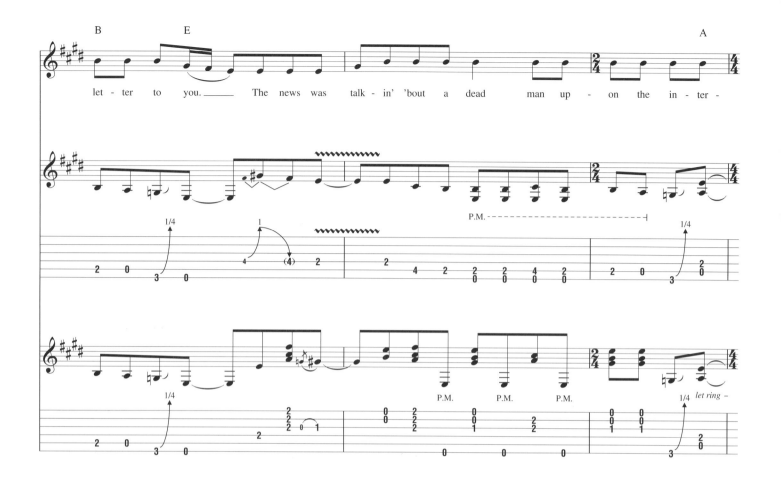

let - ter to you. _____ The news was talk - in' 'bout a dead man up - on the in - ter -

state. Seems they're look - in' for a Ca - dil - lac with

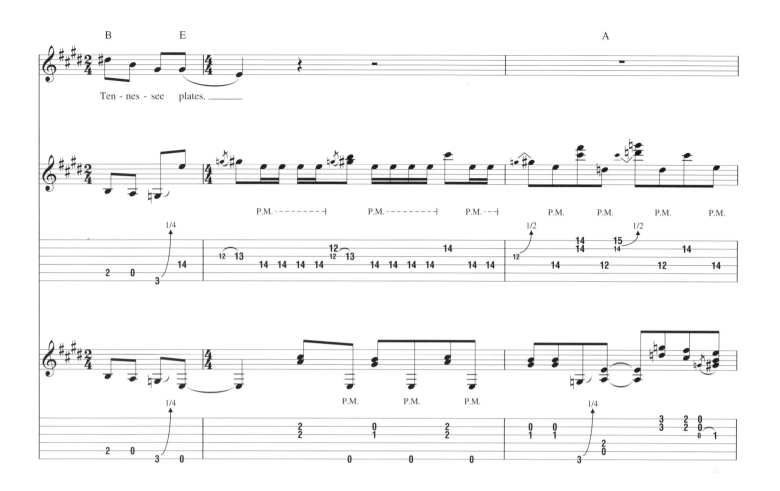

Ten - nes - see plates. _____

2. Well, since I left Cal - i - for - nia, ba - by,

things have got-ten worse. Seems the land of op-por-tu-ni-ty, for me it's just a curse. Tell that

judge in Ba-kers-field my trial -'ll have to wait. They're

looking for a Ca-dil-lac with Ten-nes-see plates. It was some-where in Ne-vad-a and cold
(It was some-where in Ne-vad-a, it was

___ out - side. ___ She was shiv-'rin' in the dark so I of-fered her a ride. Three
cold out - side.) ___

bank - jobs lat - er, four cars hot - wired, we crossed the Mis - sis - sip - pi like an oil slick fi - re!

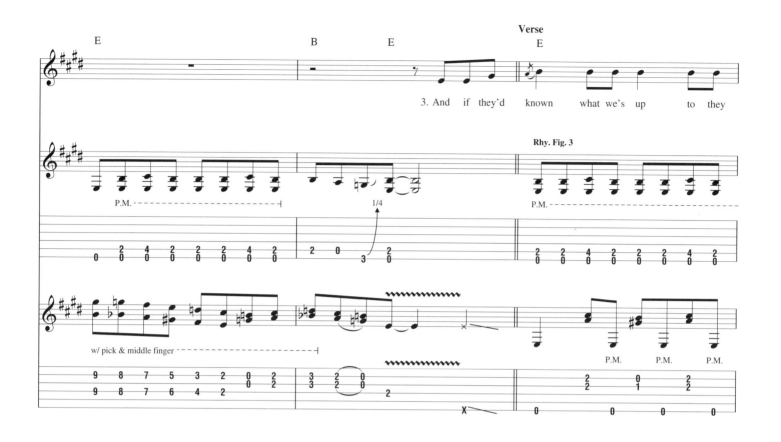

3. And if they'd known what we's up to they

would-n't have let us in. Now we land-ed in ___ Mem-phis like o - rig - i - nal sin. ___ El - vis

A

Pres - ley Boul - e - vard   to the   Grace - land   gates,   oh, _____ see, we're

E   B   E

look - in' for a   Ca - dil - lac with   Ten - nes - see   plates. _____

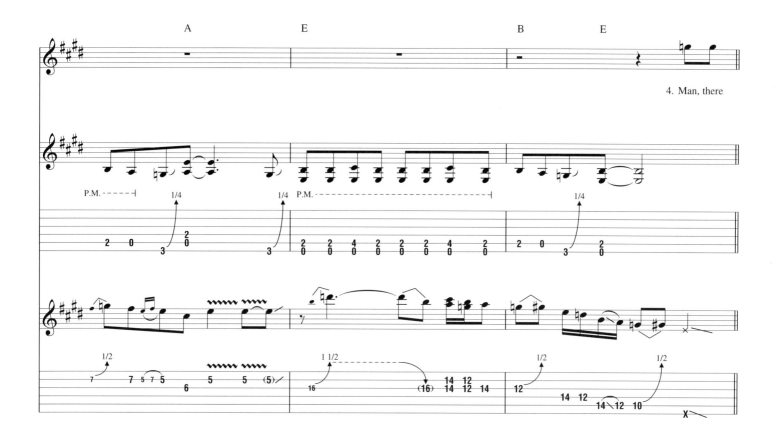

4. Man, there

Verse

must-'ve been a doz-en of 'em parked in that ga-rage. ___ There was-n't one Lin-coln and there

was-n't one Dodge. Was-n't one Jap-a-nese mod-el or make, ___

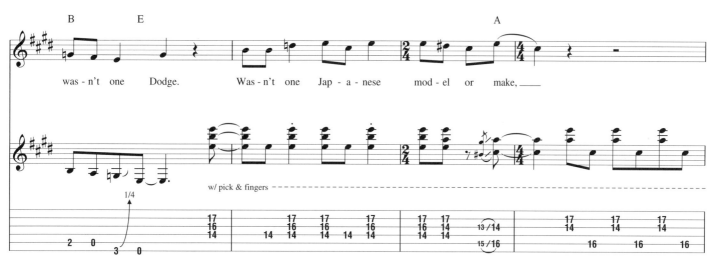

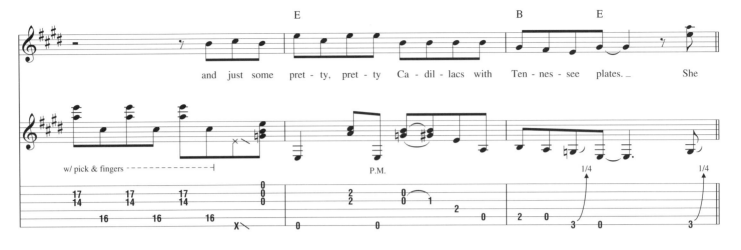

and just some pret-ty, pret-ty Ca-dil-lacs with Ten-nes-see plates. __ She

Chorus

Gtr. 2: w/ Rhy. Fig. 2

saw him sing-in' once when she was sev-en-teen. __ Ev - er since that day __ she's been

liv-in' in be-tween. __ I was nev-er king of noth-in' but that wild week-end. __ An-y-

Guitar Solo

Gtr. 2: w/ Rhy. Fig. 3 (2 times)

way, he would-n't care; hell, he gave them to his friends. __

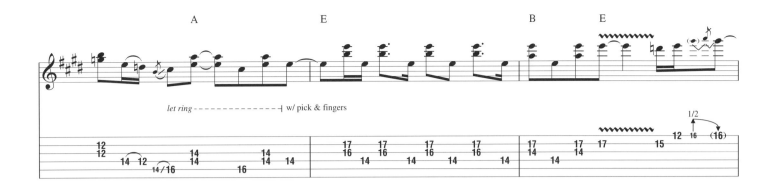

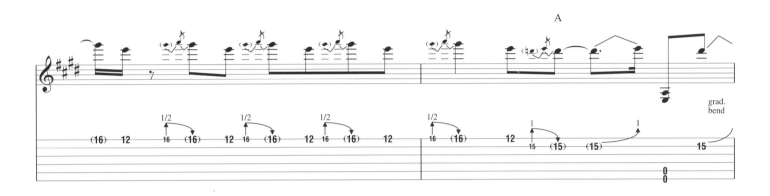

Piano Solo
Gtr. 2: w/ Rhy. Fig. 3 (2 times)

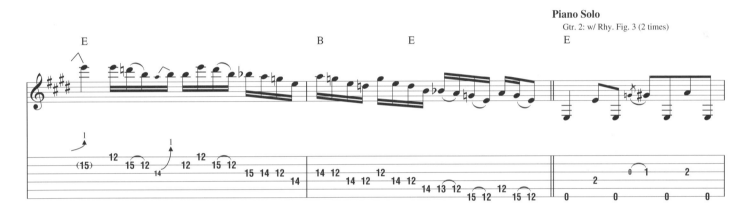

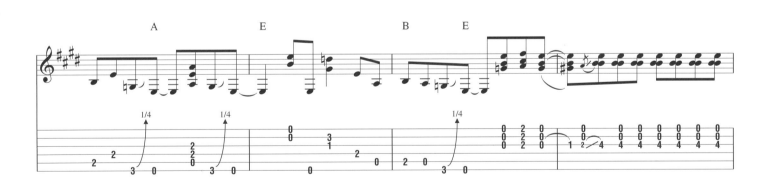

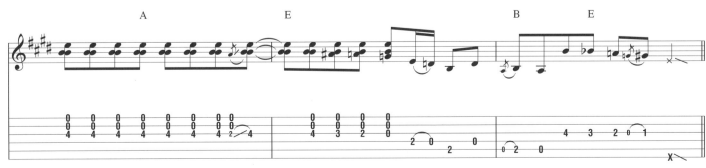

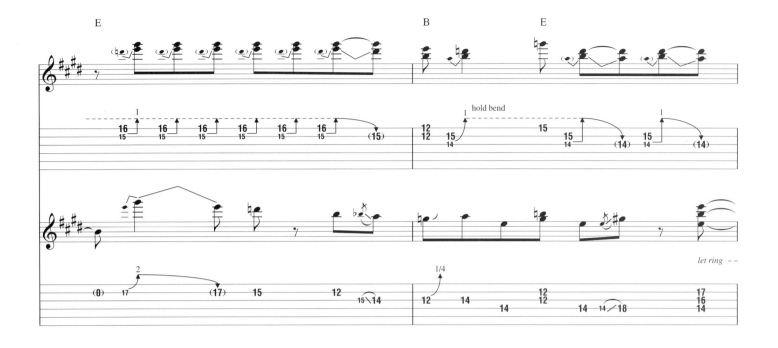

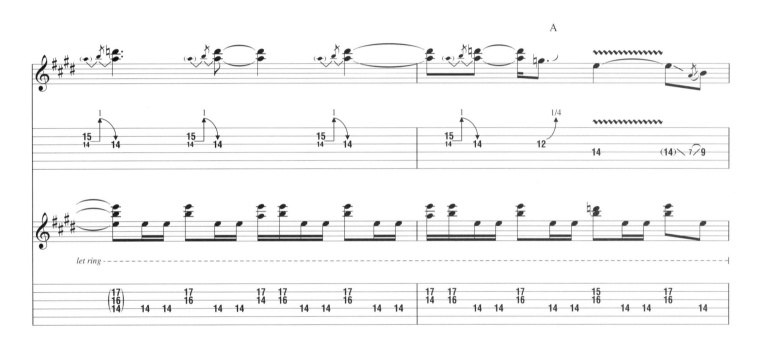

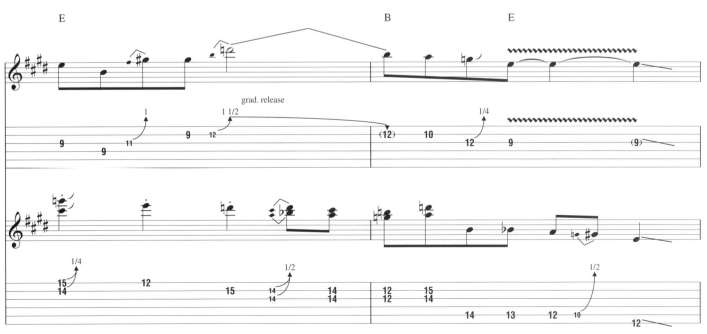

5. Ain't no ho-tel I'm writ-in' you from,

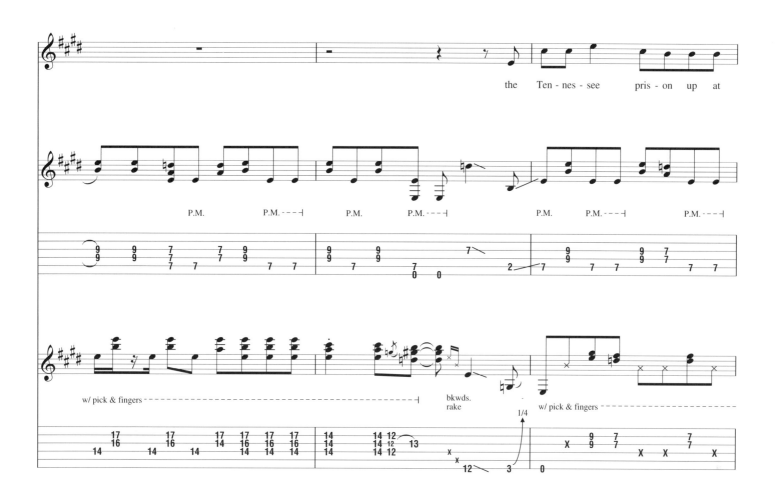

the Ten - nes - see   pris - on   up   at

Brush - y   Moun - tain, __   where

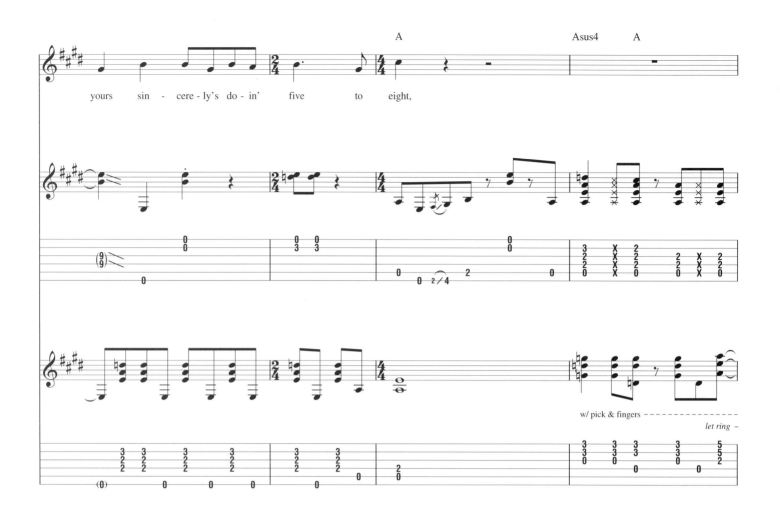

yours sin - cere - ly's do - in' five   to   eight,

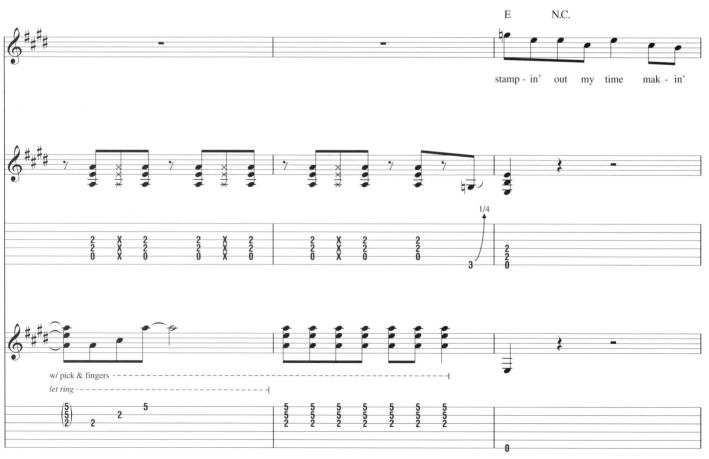

stamp - in' out my time mak - in'

Outro

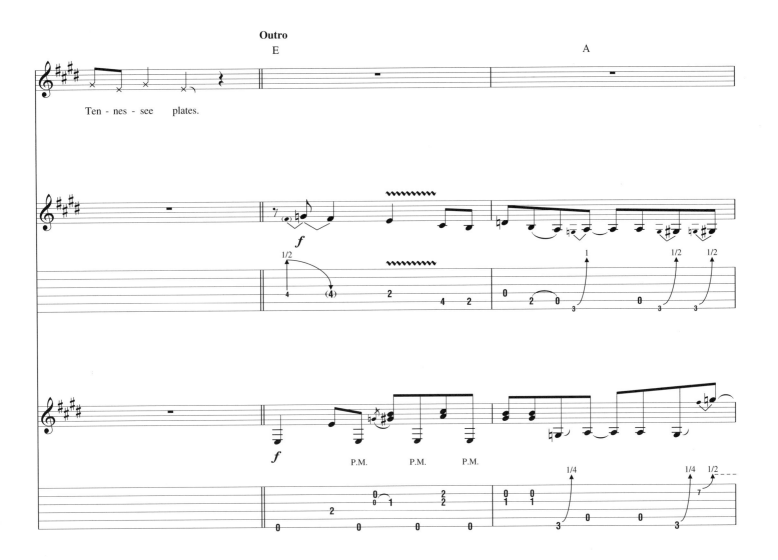

Ten - nes - see   plates.

THE MEANING OF THE BLUES

Words and Music by
Bobby Troup and Leah Worth

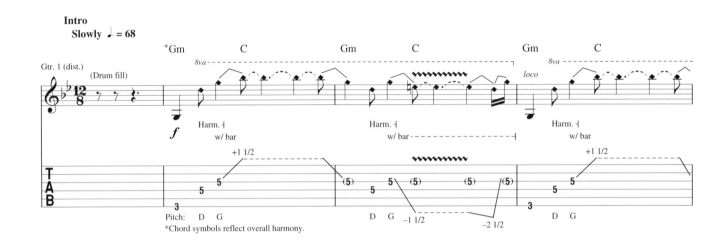

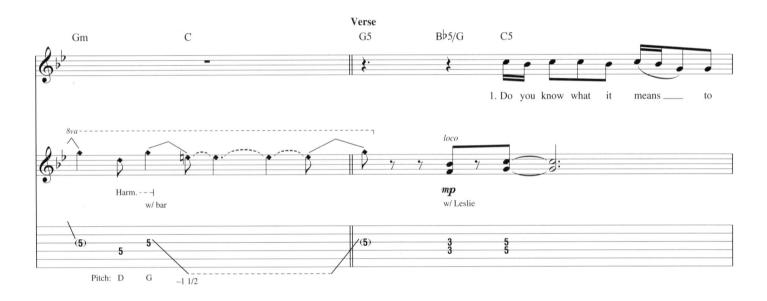

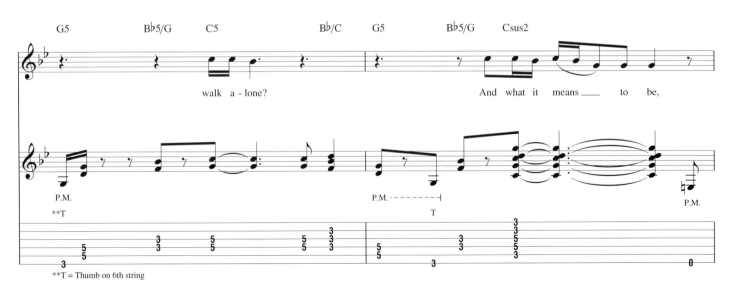

Copyright © 1957 UNIVERSAL - NORTHERN MUSIC CORPORATION and LONDONTOWN MUSIC, INC.
Copyright Renewed
All Rights Reserved   Used by Permission

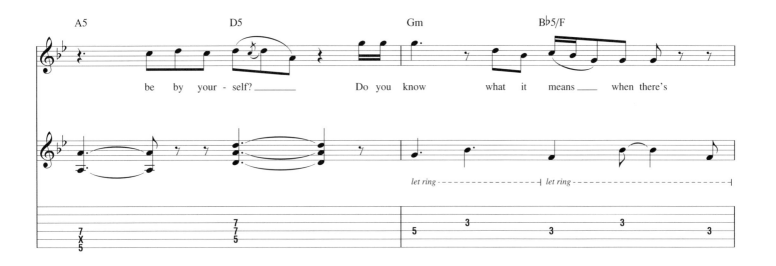

be   by   your - self?_____   Do   you   know   what   it   means ____   when   there's

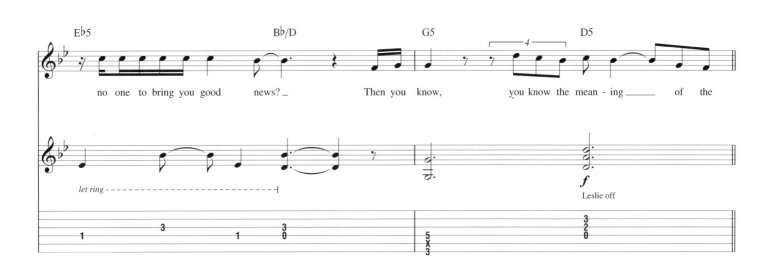

no one to bring you good   news? _   Then you   know,   you know the mean - ing _____   of the

Interlude

blues.

I've been

Bridge

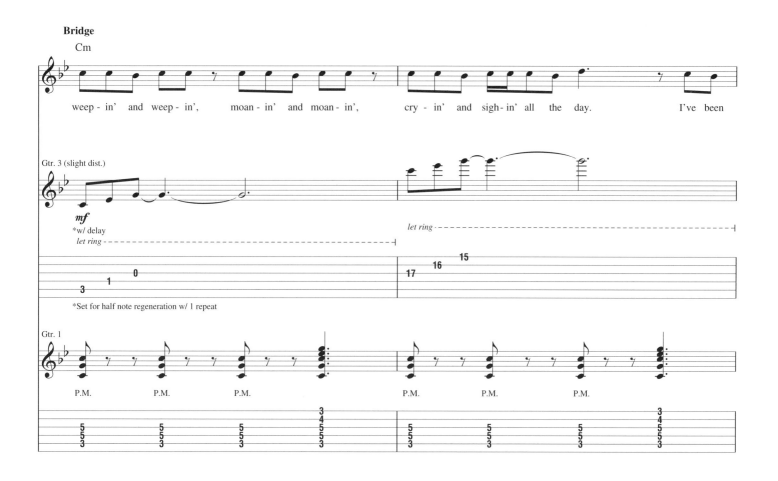

weep - in' and weep - in', moan - in' and moan - in', cry - in' and sigh - in' all the day. I've been

Gtr. 3 (slight dist.)

mf

w/ delay

let ring

let ring

*Set for half note regeneration w/ 1 repeat

Gtr. 1

P.M. P.M. P.M. P.M. P.M. P.M.

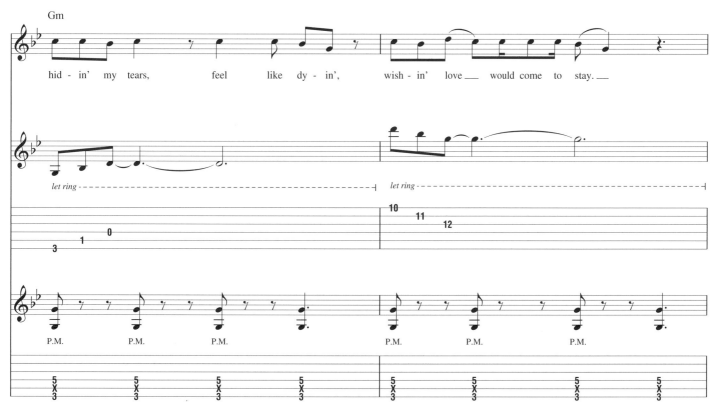

Gm

hid - in' my tears, feel like dy - in', wish - in' love ___ would come to stay. ___

let ring

let ring

P.M. P.M. P.M. P.M. P.M. P.M.

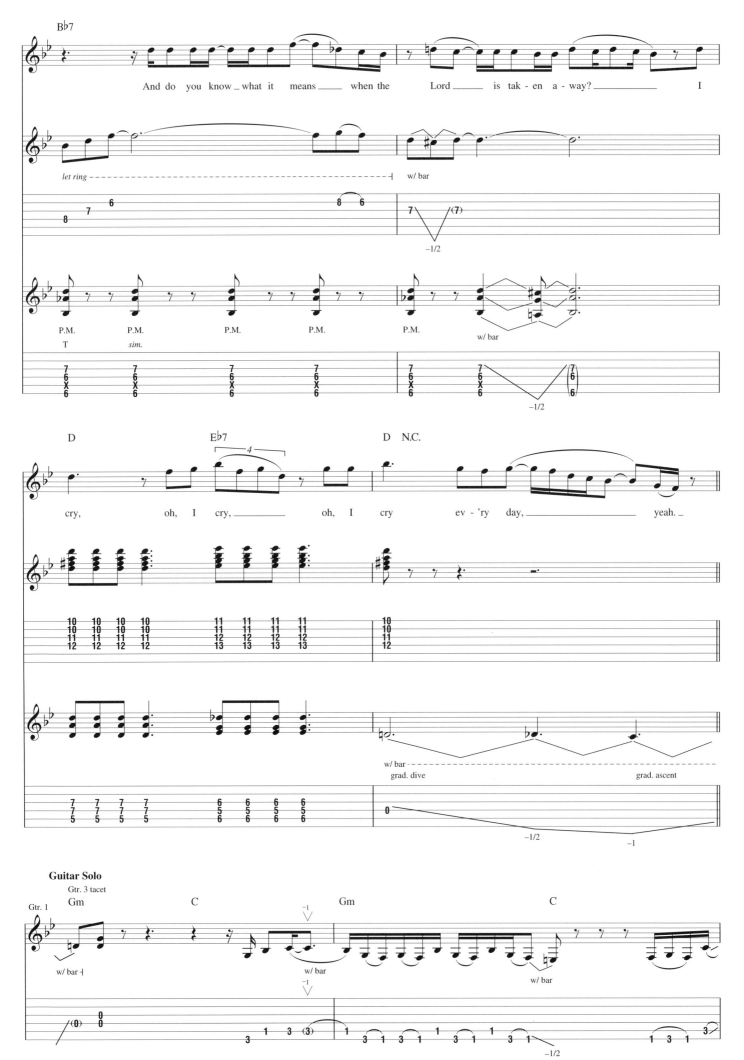

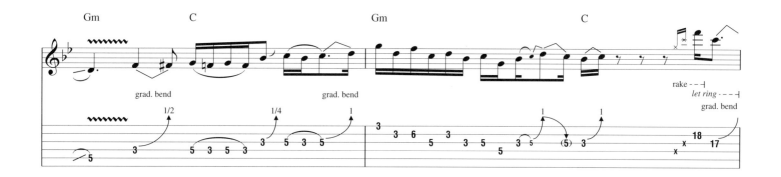

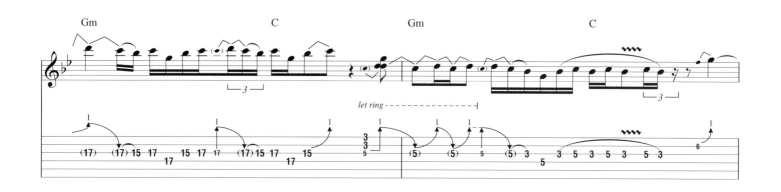

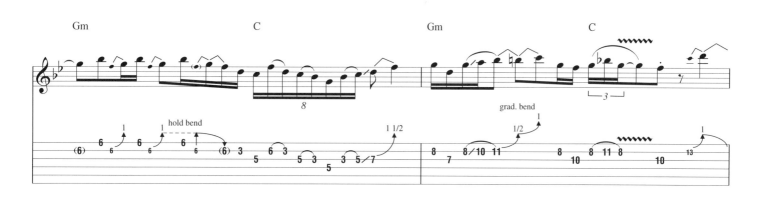

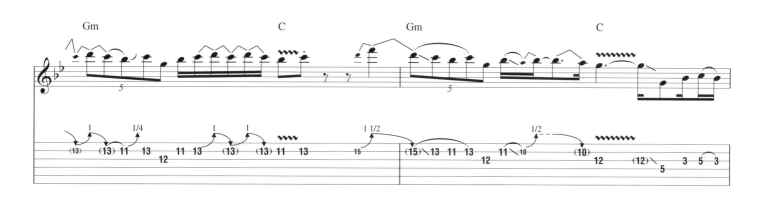

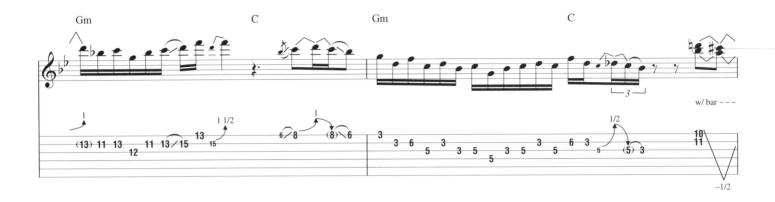

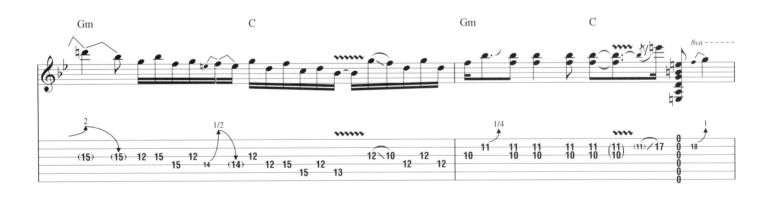

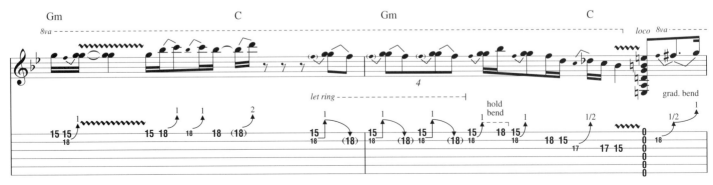

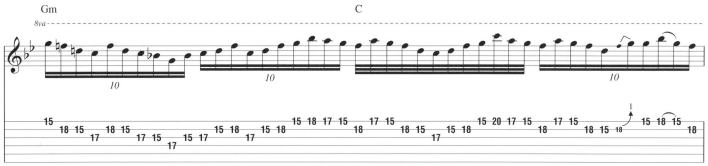

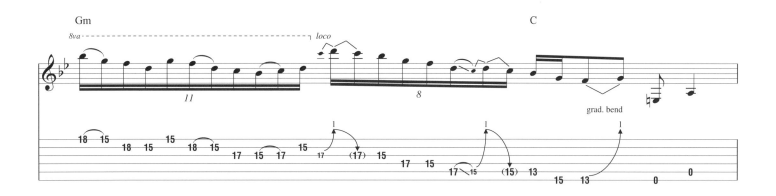

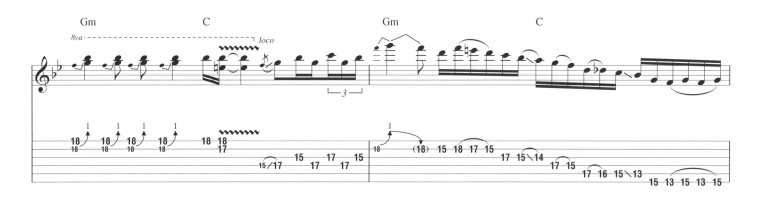

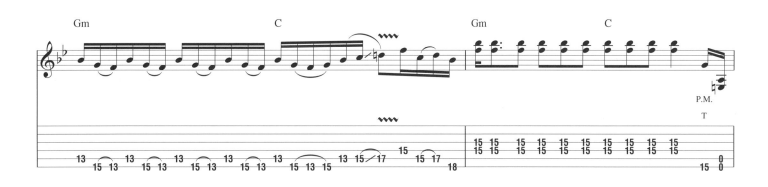

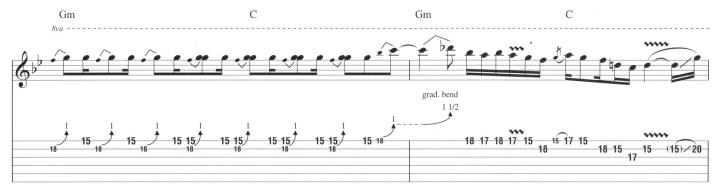

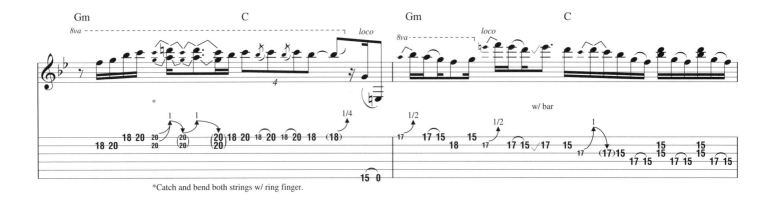

*Catch and bend both strings w/ ring finger.

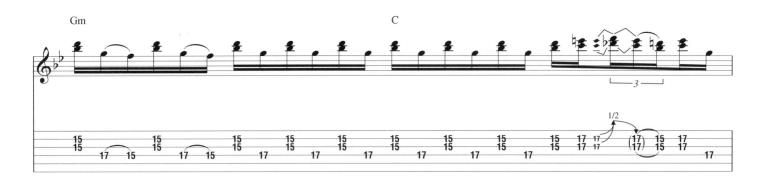

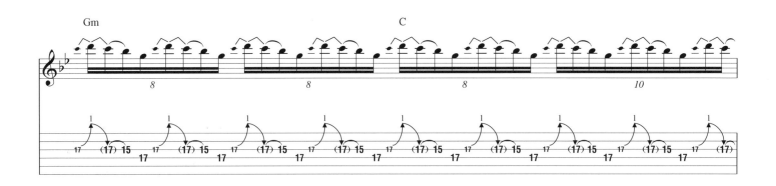

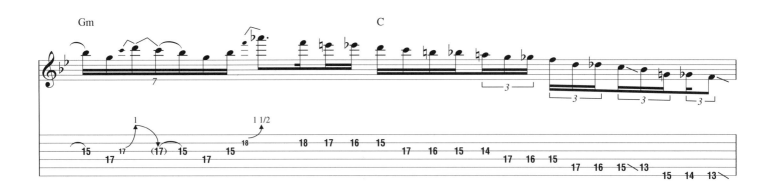

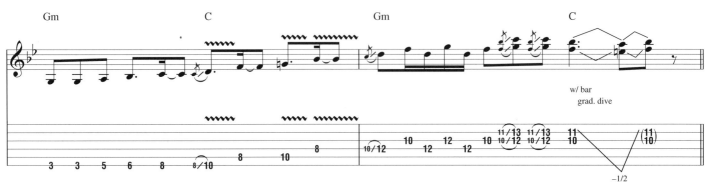

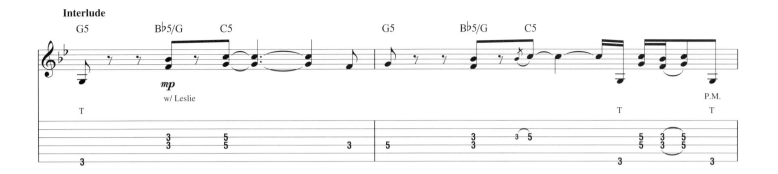

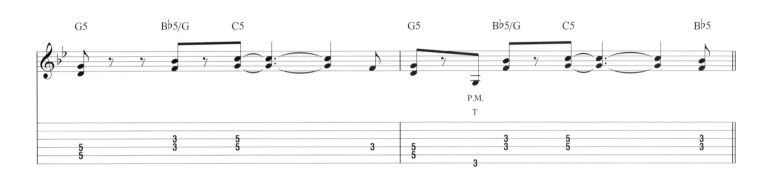

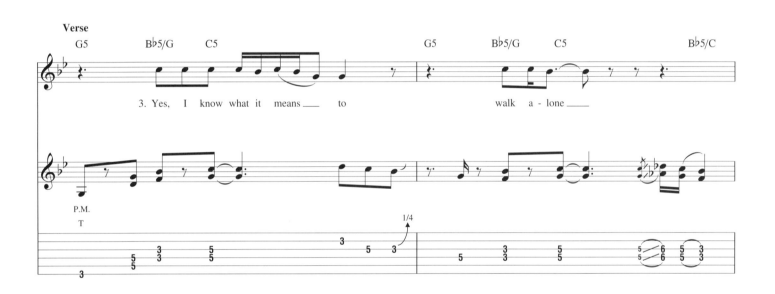

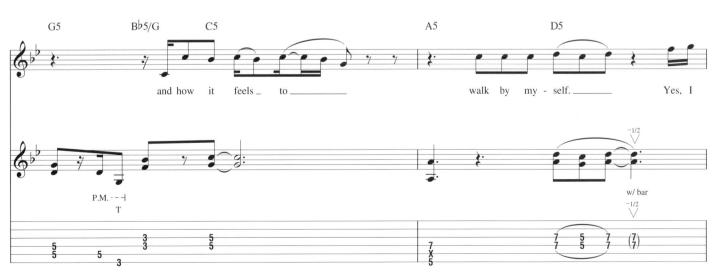

BLACK LUNG HEARTACHE

Words and Music by
Joe Bonamassa

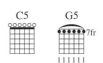

Gtrs. 1, 2, 7, 8 & 9: Tuning:
(low to high) C-G-C-G-G-C
Gtr. 5: Tune down 2 steps:
(low to high) C-F-B♭-E♭-G-C

Intro
Moderately slow ♩ = 92

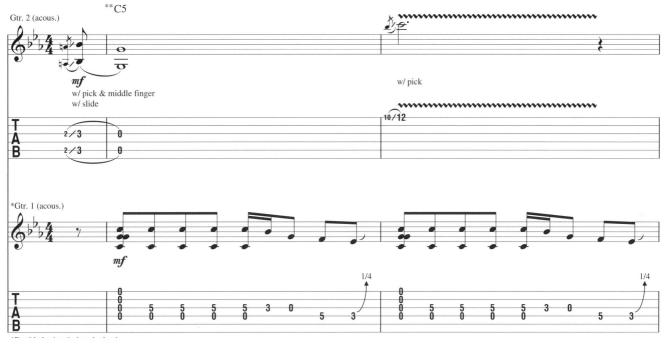

*Doubled w/ variations by banjo.

**Chord symbols reflect basic harmony.

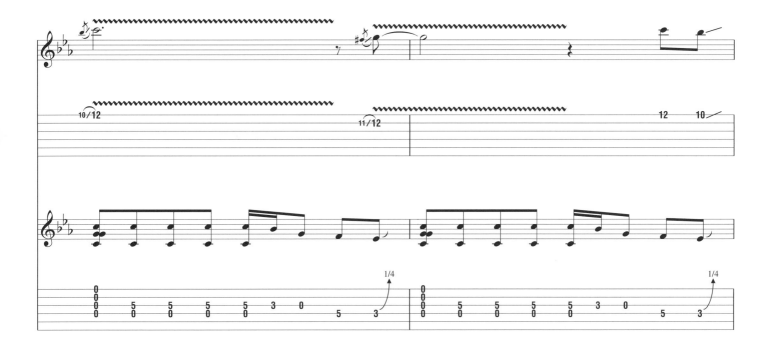

Copyright © 2011 Smokin' Joe Analog Music Co. (ASCAP)
International Copyright Secured   All Rights Reserved

Verse

Gtr. 1: w/ Rhy. Fig. 1 (2 times)

C5

2. I sleep in a mod - est ____ house, ____

these green hills ____ I mind. ____ And if I

steady gliss. *steady gliss.*

die, who'll tend ____ my chil - dren? Who will be ____ by their side? ____

*Two gtrs. arr. for one

**Symbols in parentheses represent chord names respective
to Gtr. 5. Symbols above reflect actual sounding chords.

***Vol. swell

Interlude

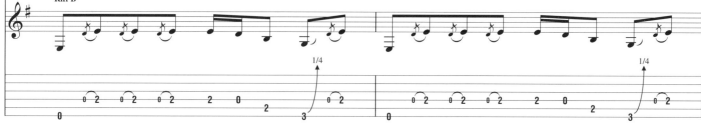

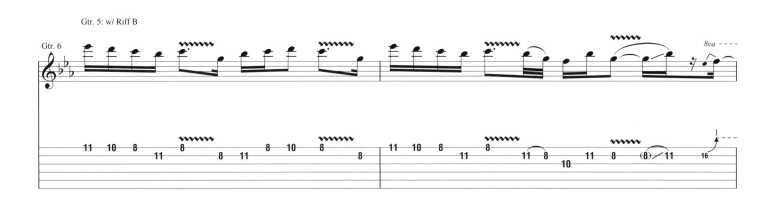

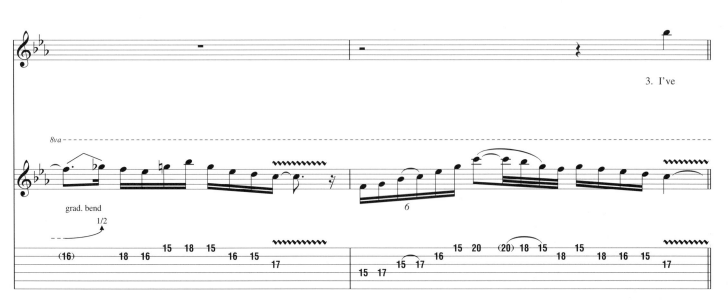

hang   on, _____   hang   on. _____   Black   lung   heart - ache. _____

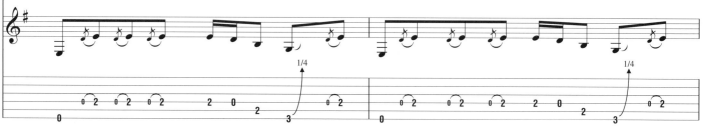

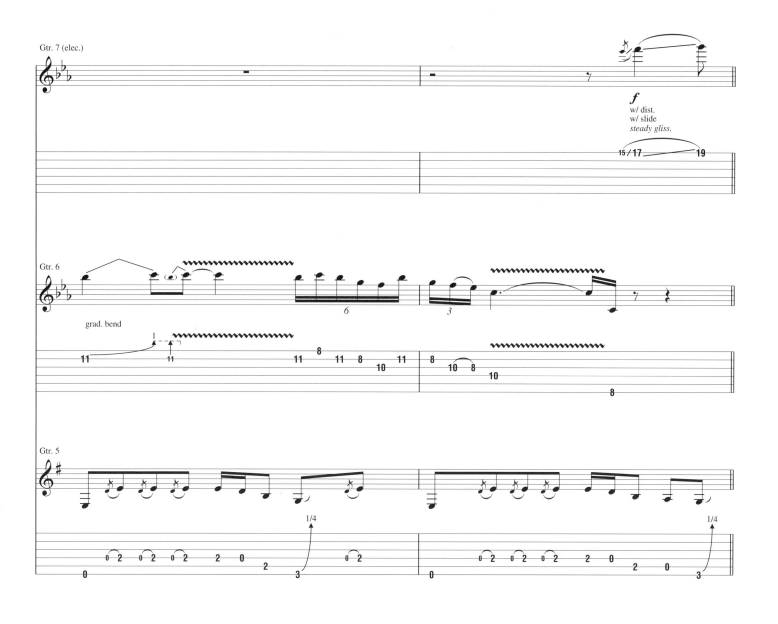

Guitar Solo

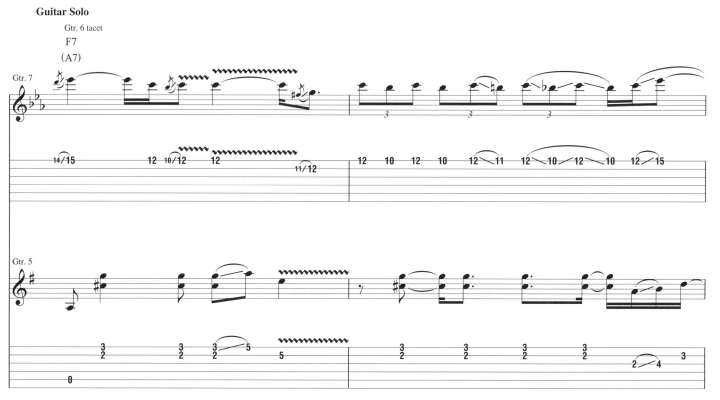

73

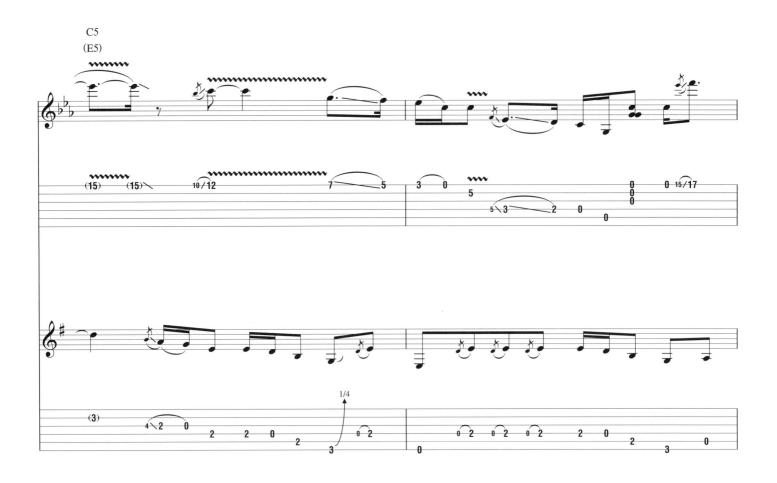

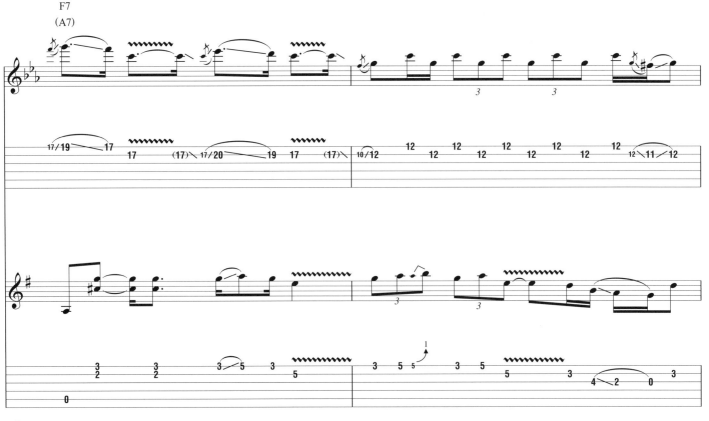

Interlude

Gtrs. 1, 3 & 4: w/ Riffs A, A1 & A2
Gtrs. 5 & 8 tacet

4. I've seen

Gtr. 1: w/ Rhy. Fig. 2

Now, I said so long,___ so long.___ Black lung heart - ache.___

w/ pick & middle finger
steady gliss.

Outro
Gtr. 1: w/ Riff A (1 3/4 times)
Gtr. 2 tacet
Gtrs. 3 & 4: w/ Riffs A1 & A2 (1 1/2 times)

YOU BETTER WATCH YOURSELF

Words and Music by
Walter Jacobs

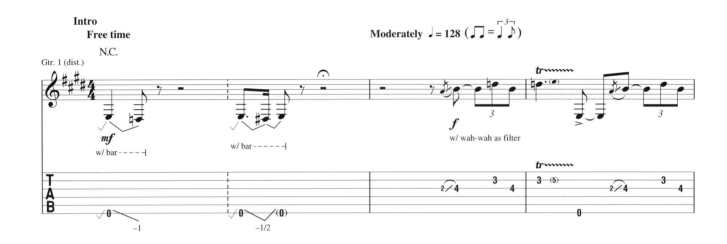

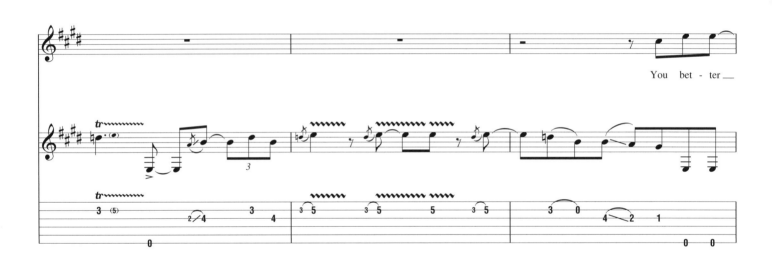

*Chord symbols reflect basic harmony.

Copyright © 1959 (Renewed) by Arc Music Corporation (BMI)
All Rights Administered by BMG Chrysalis
International Copyright Secured   All Rights Reserved
Used by Permission

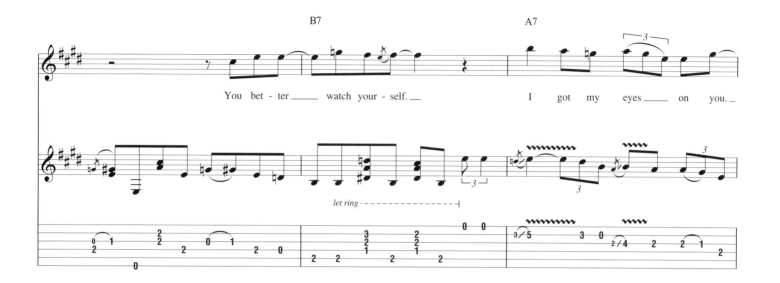

You bet - ter _____ watch your - self. _____   I got my eyes _____ on you. __

Guitar Solo

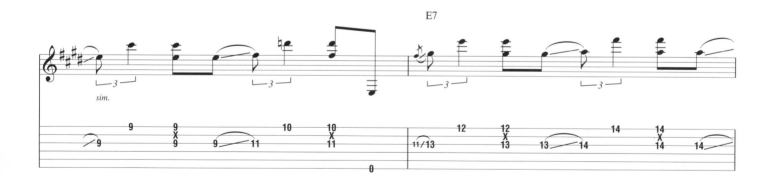

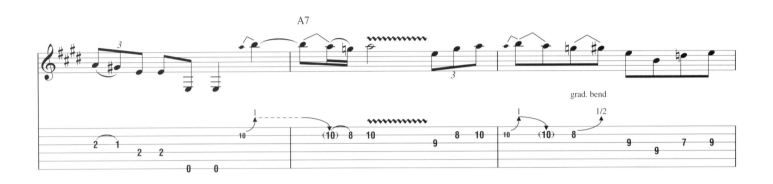

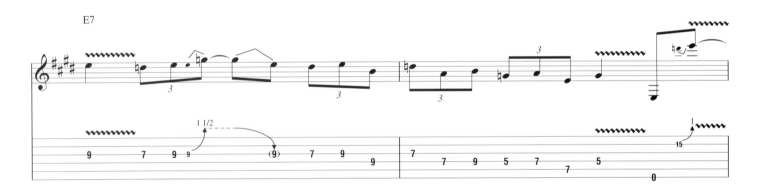

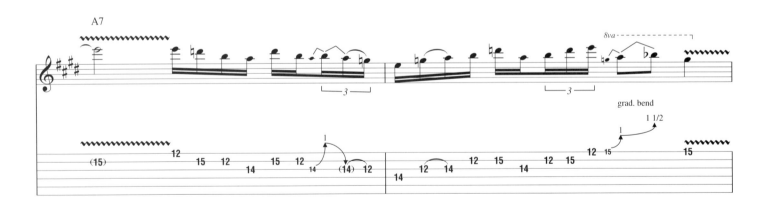

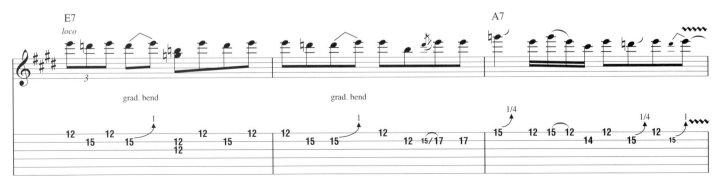

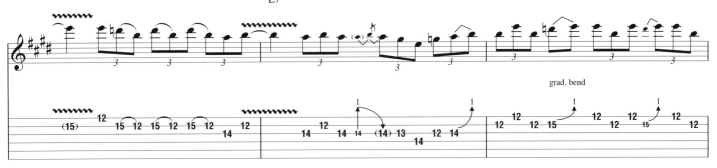

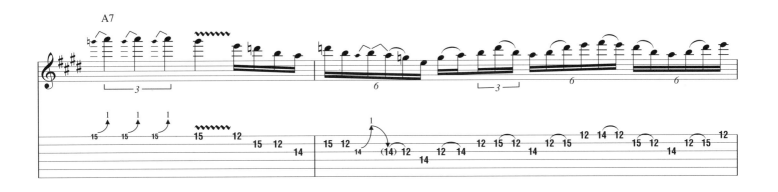

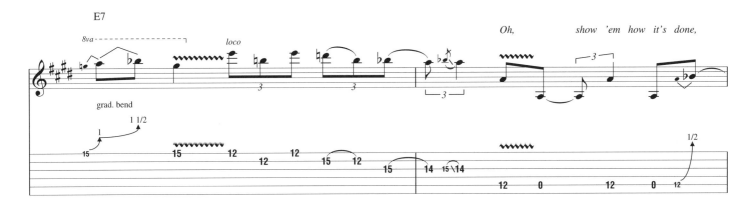

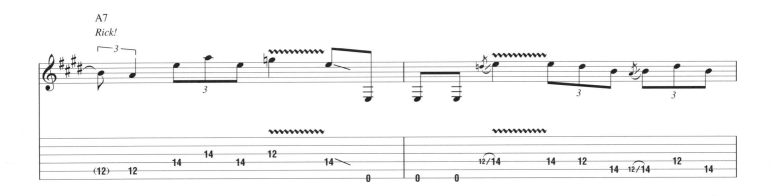

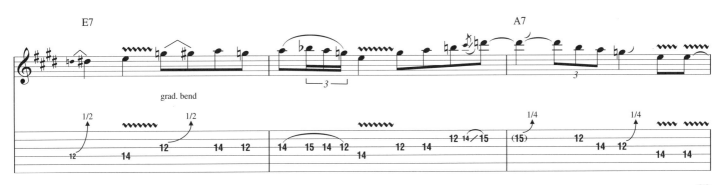

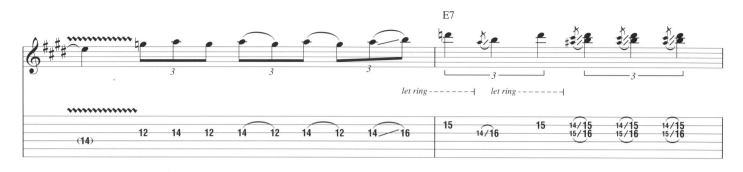

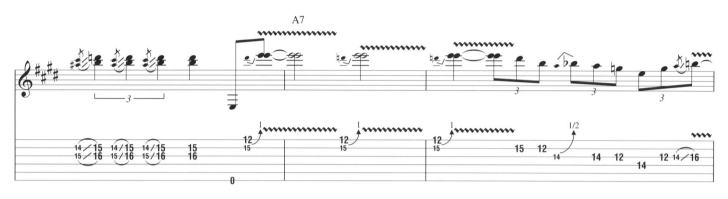

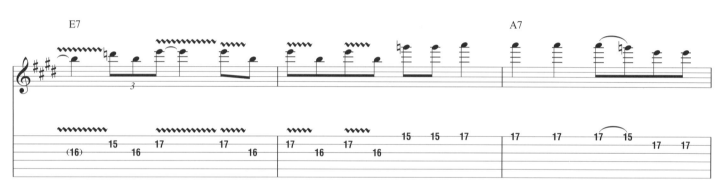

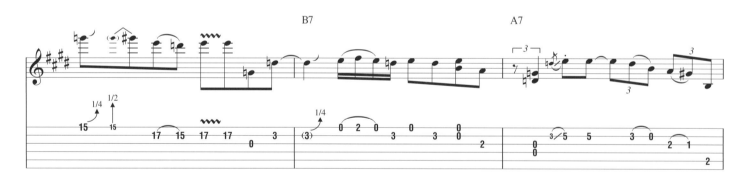

3. Well,

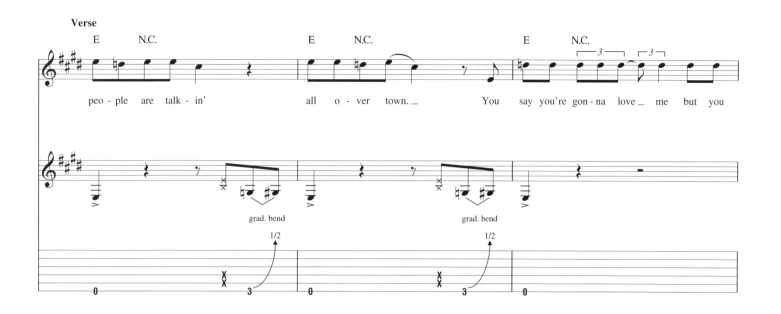

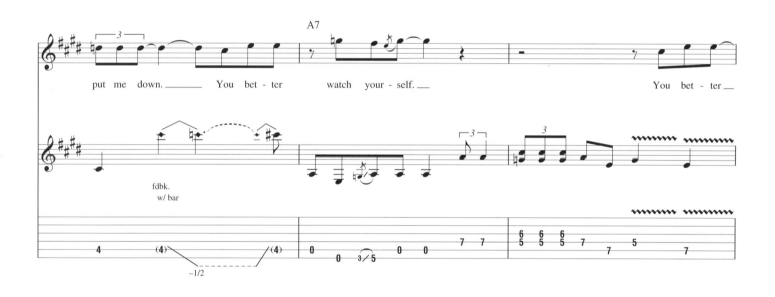

I got my eyes ___ on you. ___ Yeah. ___

Outro

N.C.

Free time

D5 N.C.

Hey, yeah, ___ yeah. ___

Mm. ___

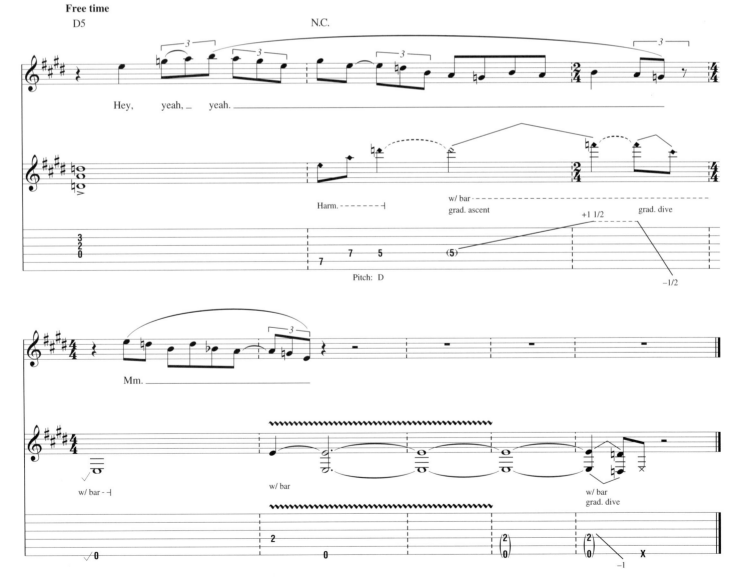

THE LAST MATADOR OF BAYONNE

Words and Music by
Joe Bonamassa

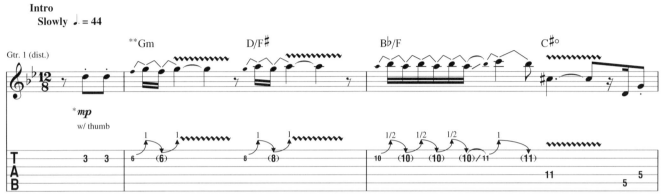

*Begin song w/ gtr.'s vol. knob lowered approximately halfway, thereby reducing dist. level.

**Chord symbols reflect overall harmony.

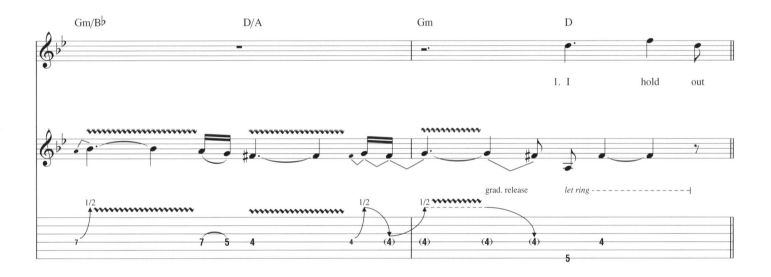

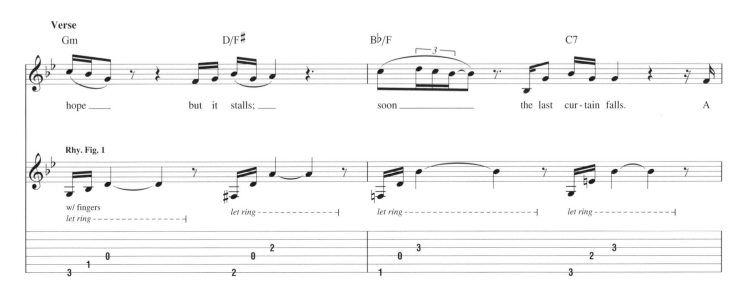

Copyright © 2011 Smokin' Joe Analog Music Co. (ASCAP)
International Copyright Secured   All Rights Reserved

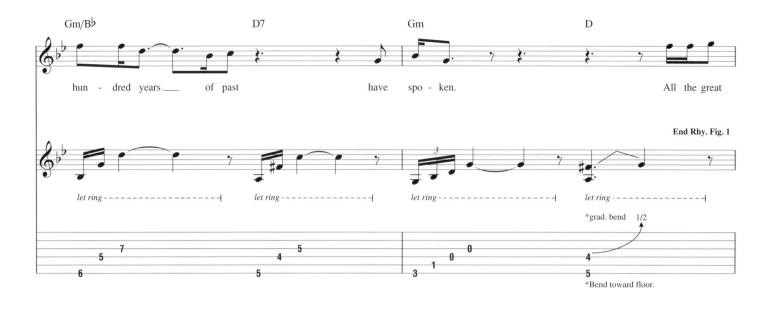

hun - dred years ___ of past have spo - ken. All the great

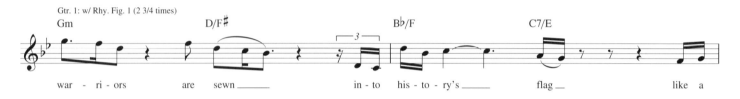

war - ri - ors are sewn ___ in - to his - to - ry's ___ flag ___ like a

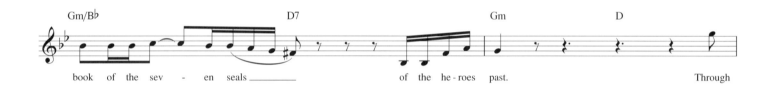

book of the sev - en seals ___ of the he - roes past. Through

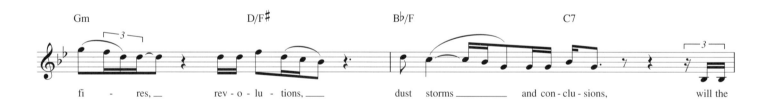

fi - res, ___ rev - o - lu - tions, ___ dust storms ___ and con - clu - sions, will the

show _ go on ___ to - night ___ one more time? I fight on, ___ fight on; ___ I'm the

last mat - a - dor ___ of Bay - onne, for to - mor - row this place ___ falls ___ in - to

Guitar Solo

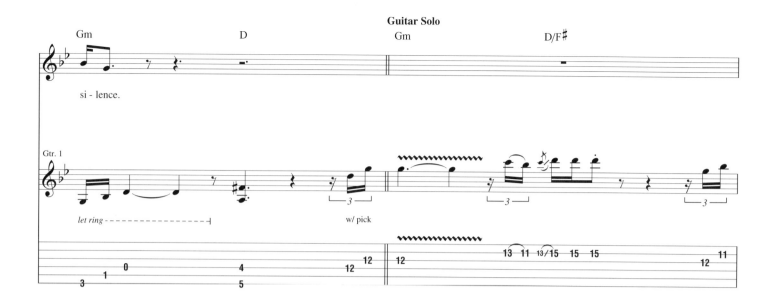

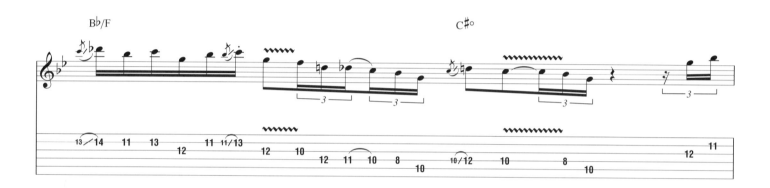

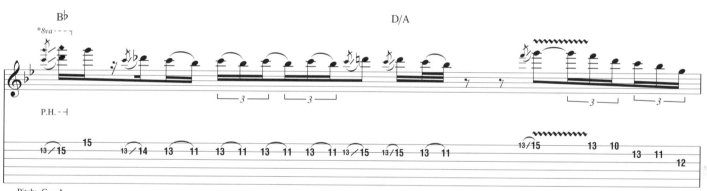

Pitch: G   A

*Refers to harmonics only

**Raise to full vol. w/ gtr.'s knob.

89

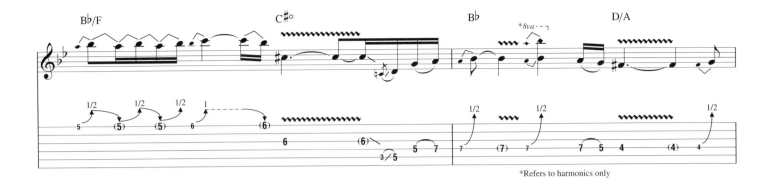

*Refers to harmonics only

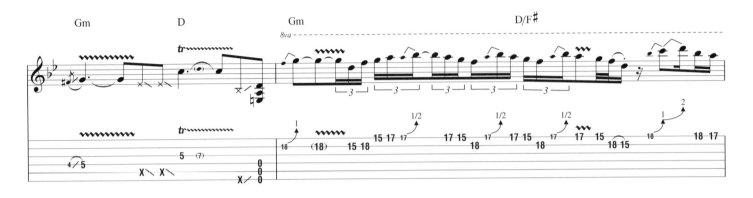

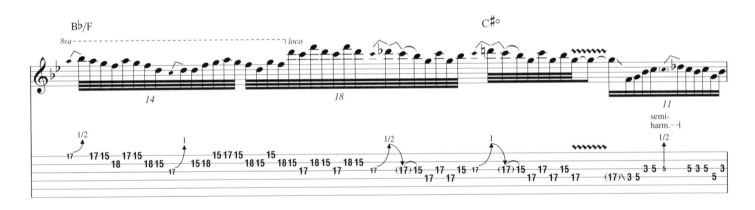

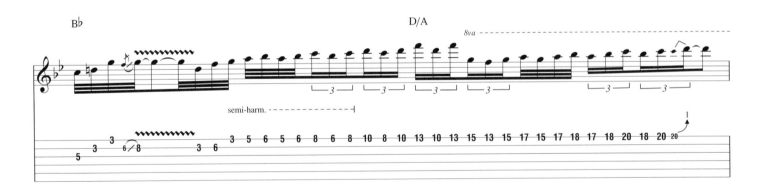

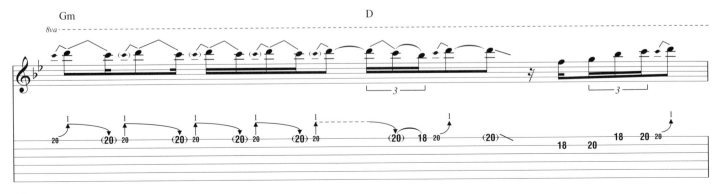

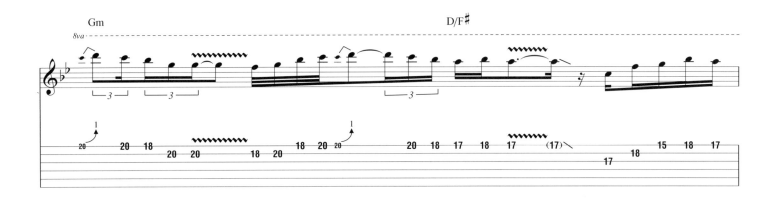

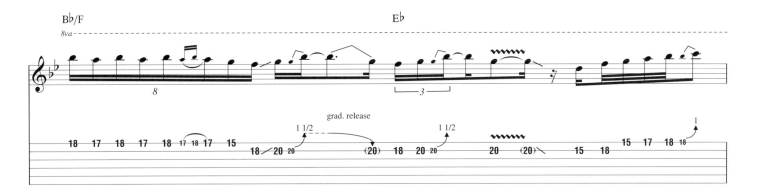

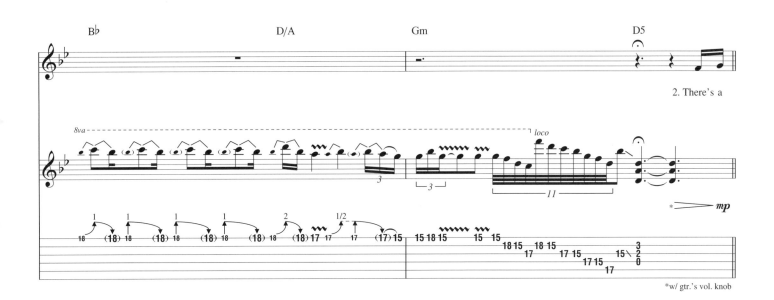

*w/ gtr.'s vol. knob

Verse

Gtr. 1: w/ Rhy. Fig. 1 (1 1/2 times)

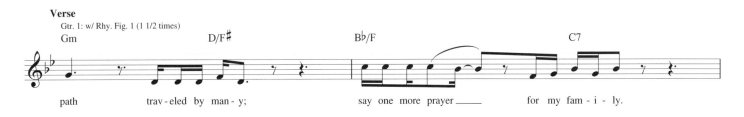

path trav-eled by man-y; say one more prayer _____ for my fam-i-ly.

Like a ship _ with-out _____ a sail _____ cast a-drift, I fight

on, _____ fight on; _____ I'm the last mat-a-dor _____ of Bay-onne. A

hun-dred years ____ of past _____ now are gone.

Outro

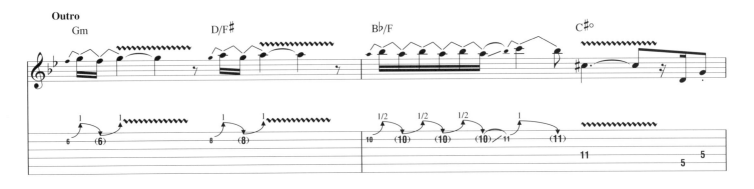

Free time

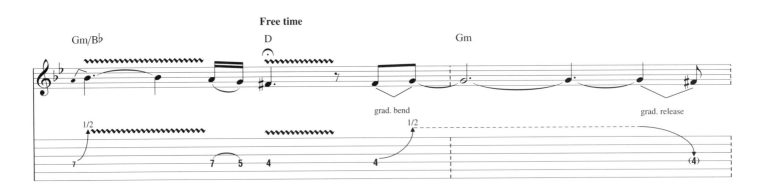

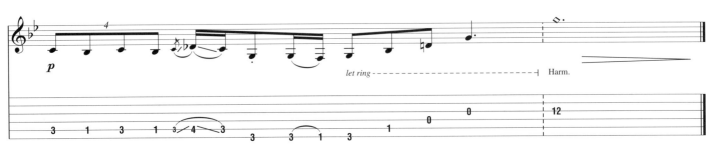

HEARTBREAKER

Words and Music by
Paul Rodgers

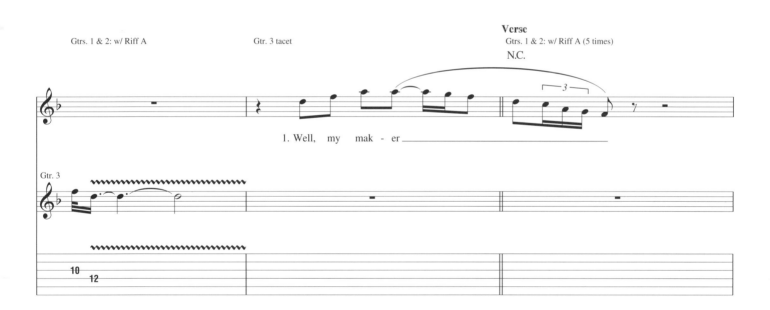

1. Well, my mak-er _____ must-'ve been a hard heart-break-er, _____ and I'll tell you why.

Copyright © 1972 Keepers Cottage Music Ltd.
Copyright Renewed
All Rights in the United States and Canada Controlled and Administered by UNIVERSAL - POLYGRAM INTERNATIONAL PUBLISHING, INC.
All Rights Reserved   Used by Permission

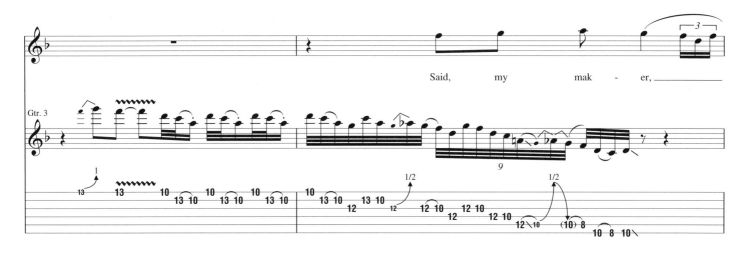

Said, my mak - er, _____

_____ uh,   must - 've been a hard   heart -

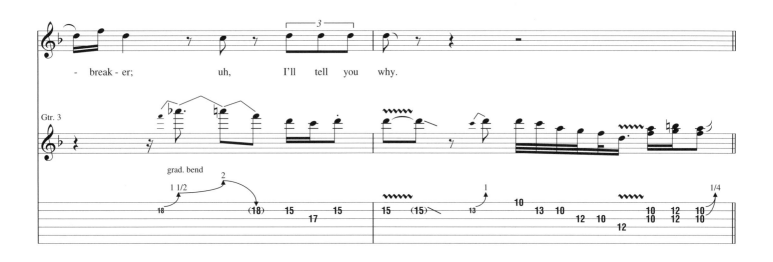

- break - er;   uh,   I'll tell you why.

Chorus

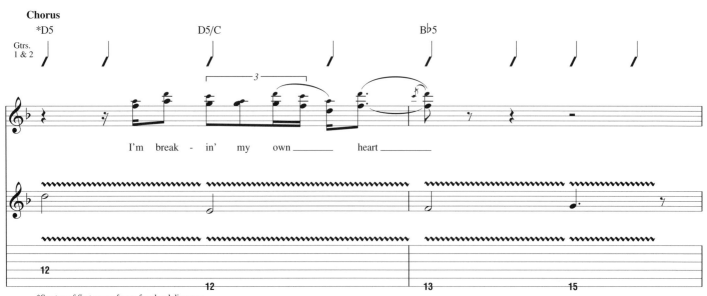

I'm break - in' my own _____ heart _____

*See top of first page of song for chord diagrams
pertaining to rhythm slashes.

94

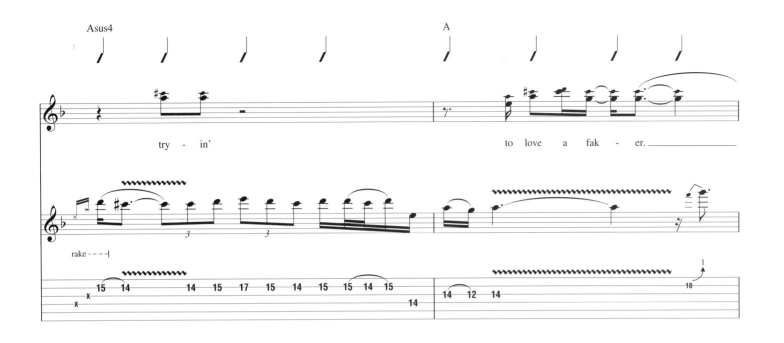

try - in'
to love a fak - er.

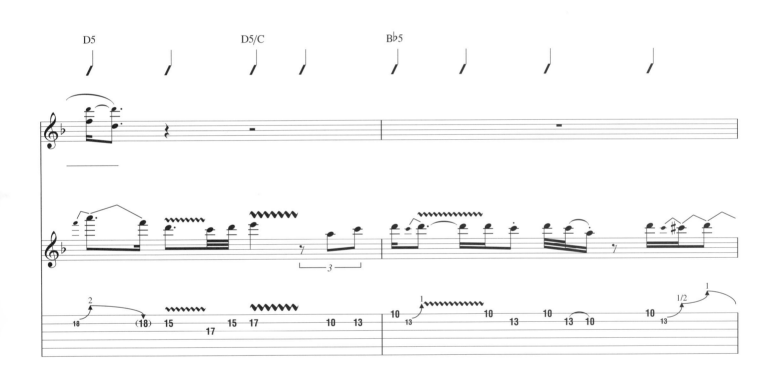

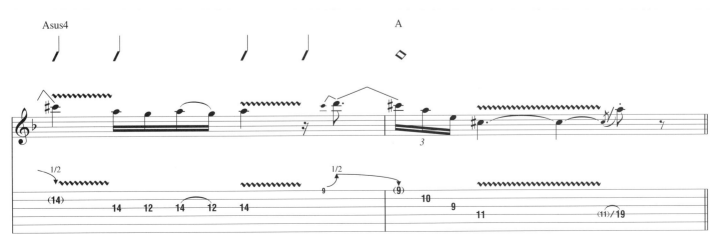

Interlude

Gtrs. 1 & 2: w/ Riff A (2 times)
Gtr. 3 tacet

And I'll tell your soul. _____ Mm. _____

2. Just like a blind, _____ blind _____

Gtr. 3

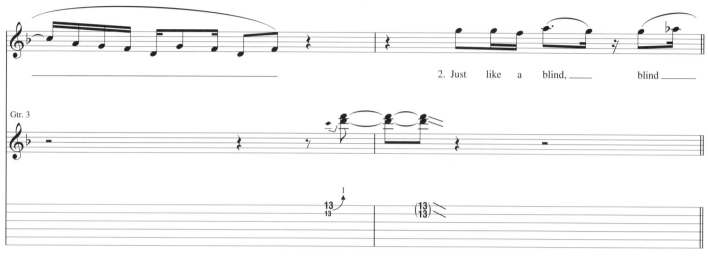

Verse

Gtrs. 1 & 2: w/ Riff A (5 times)

man, _____ my lit - tle house is on _____

Gtr. 3 tacet

_____ fi - re. _____ Mm. _____

Just like a blind _____

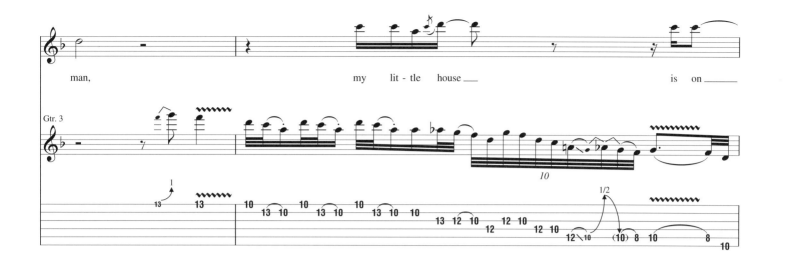

man, my lit - tle house _____ is on _____

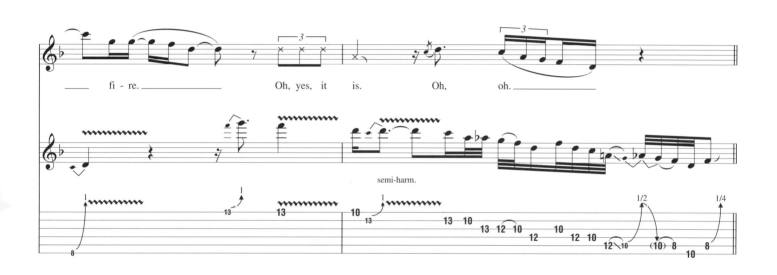

_____ fi - re. _____ Oh, yes, it is. Oh, oh. _____

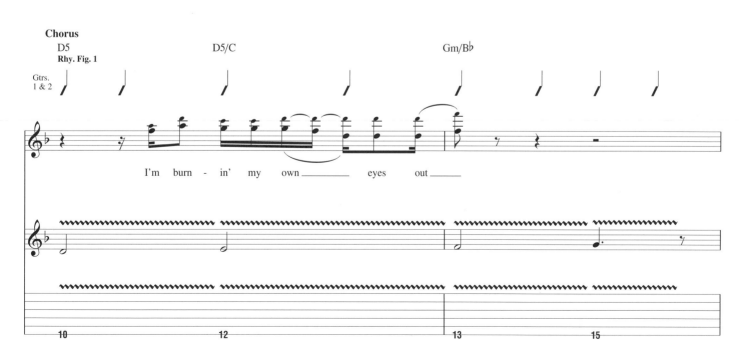

Chorus

I'm burn - in' my own _____ eyes out _____

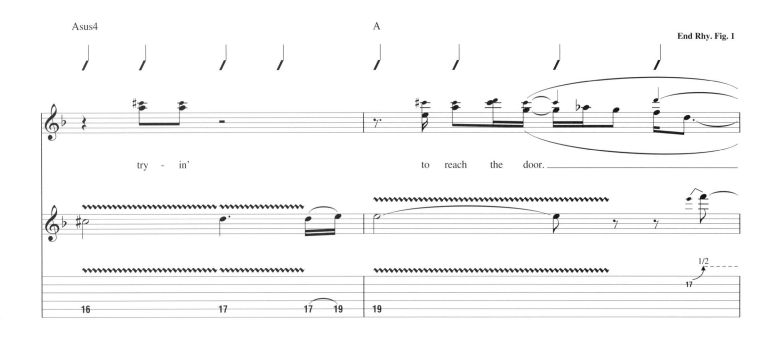

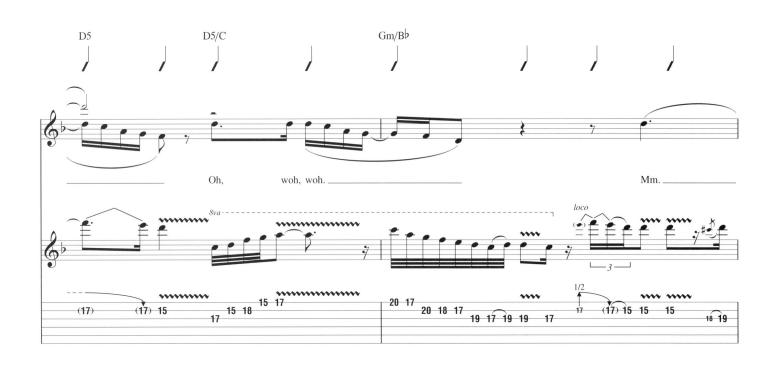

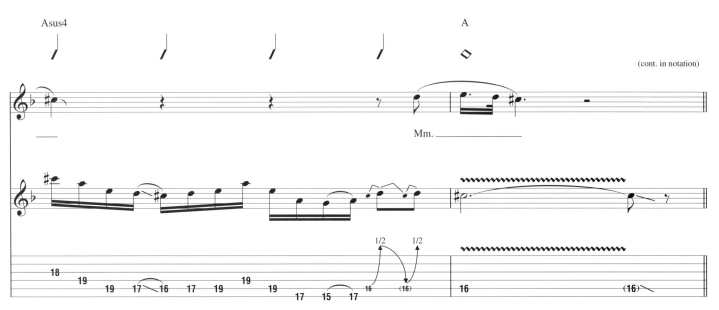

98

Guitar Solo

Riff B

End Riff B

Gtrs. 1 & 2: w/ Riff B

Gtr. 2: w/ Riff B (2 times)

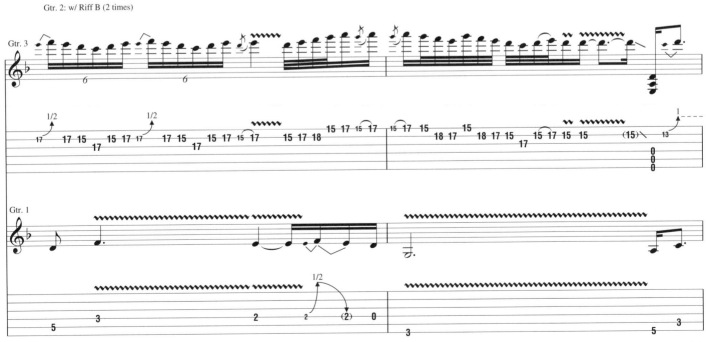

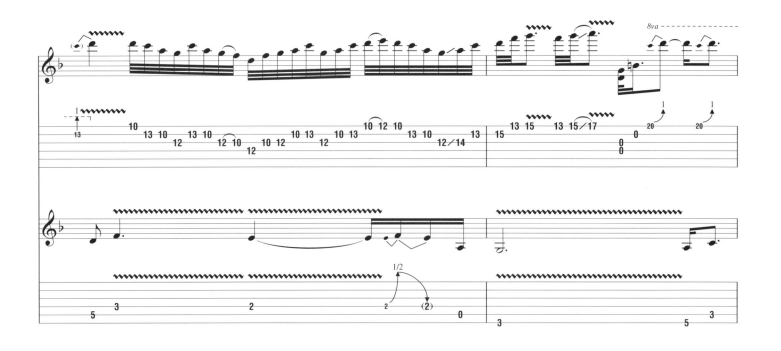

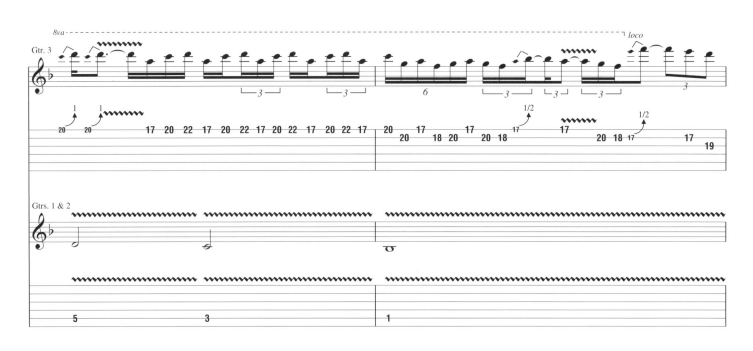

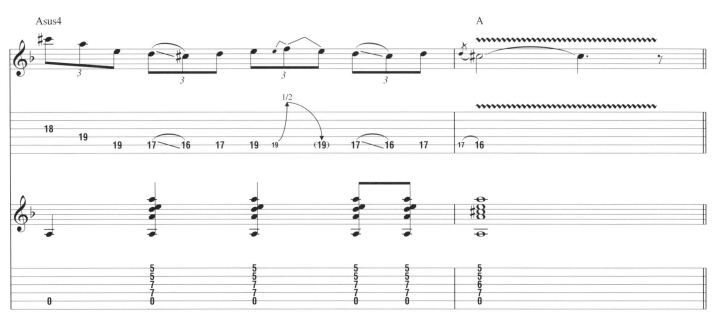

Interlude

Gtrs. 1 & 2: w/ Riff A (3 times)

N.C.

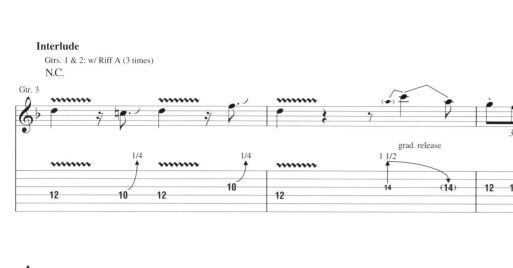

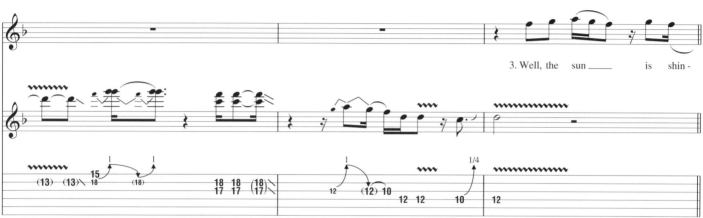

3. Well, the sun ____ is shin-

Verse

Gtrs. 1 & 2: w/ Riff A (5 times)

N.C.

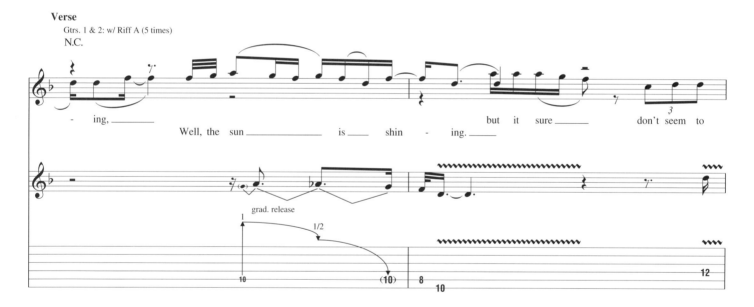

-ing, ____ Well, the sun ____ is ____ shin - ing. ____ but it sure ____ don't seem to

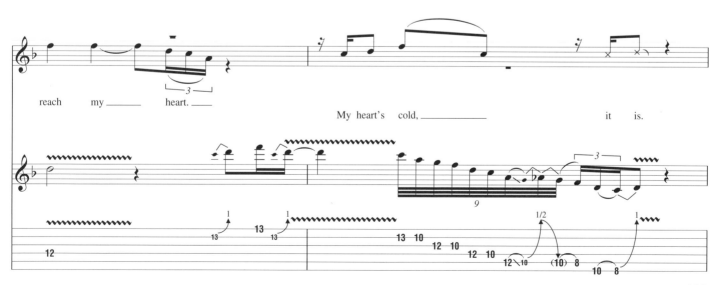

reach my ____ heart. ____ My heart's cold, _____ it is.

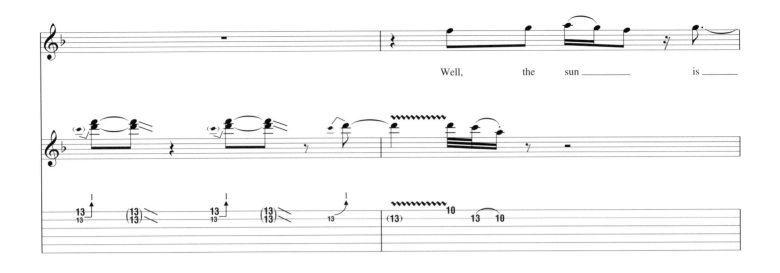

Well,　　　the　sun＿＿＿＿＿　is＿＿＿＿

＿＿ shin - ing,＿＿＿　　but　it　sure＿＿＿＿　　don't　seem　to

Well, the sun＿＿＿＿＿ is　shin - ing.＿＿＿＿

reach　　my＿＿＿＿＿　heart.＿＿　　　　　　　　　　　　　　My　heart　is　cold.

Reach　　my　heart.＿＿＿＿＿＿＿＿　　My　heart　is　cold.＿

Chorus

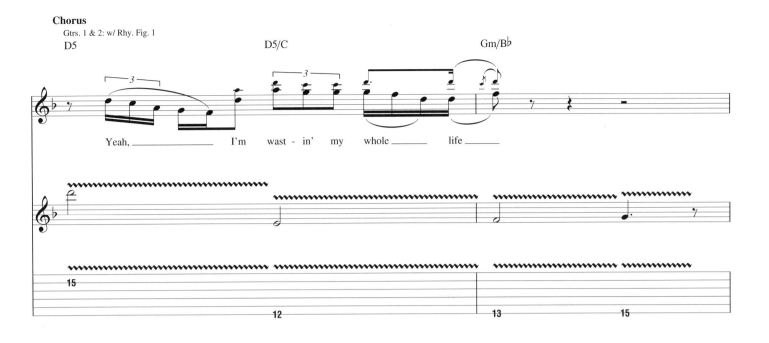

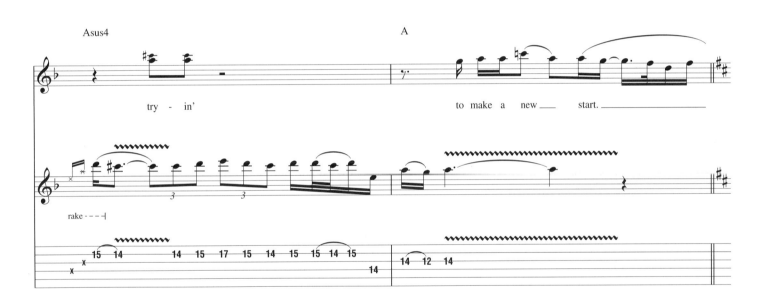

Outro

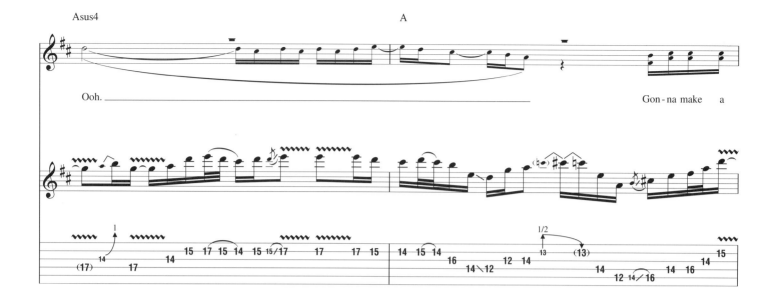

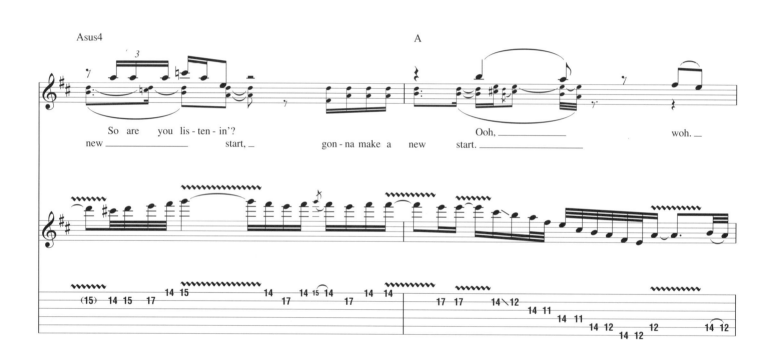

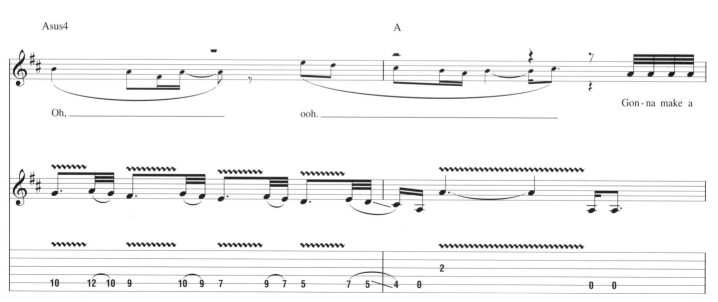

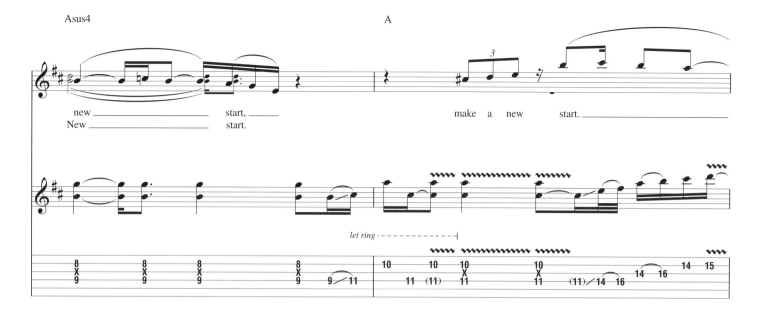

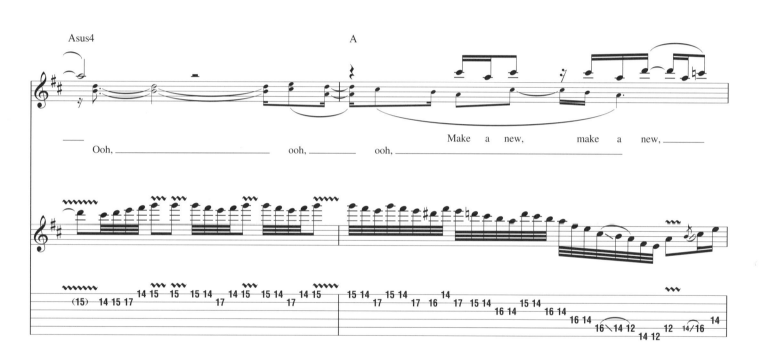

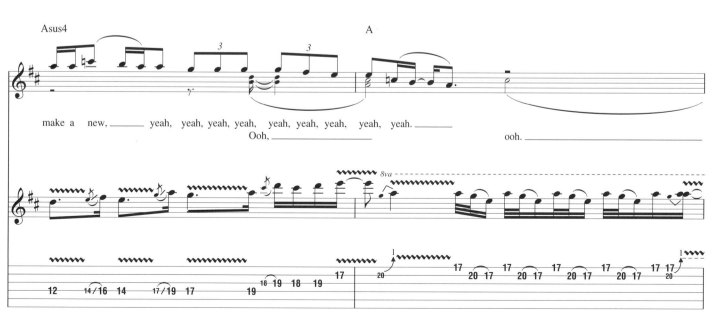

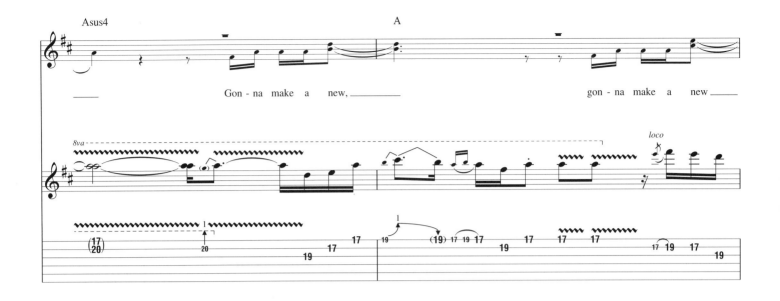

Gon - na make a new, _____ gon - na make a new _____

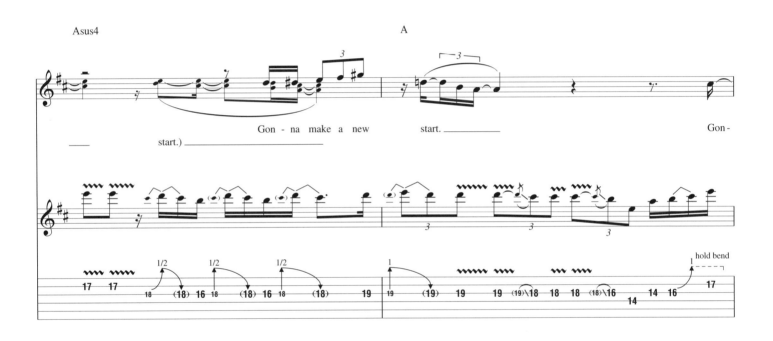

Gon - na make a new start. _____ Gon -

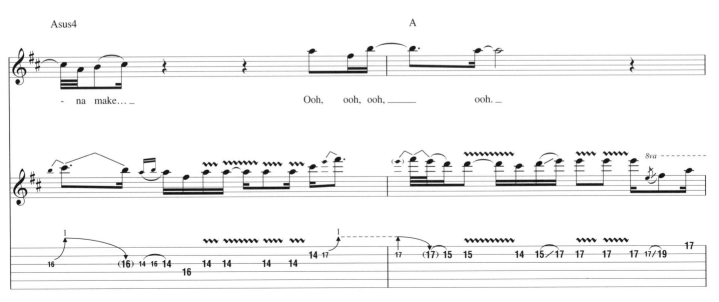

- na make… _____ Ooh, ooh, ooh, _____ ooh. _____

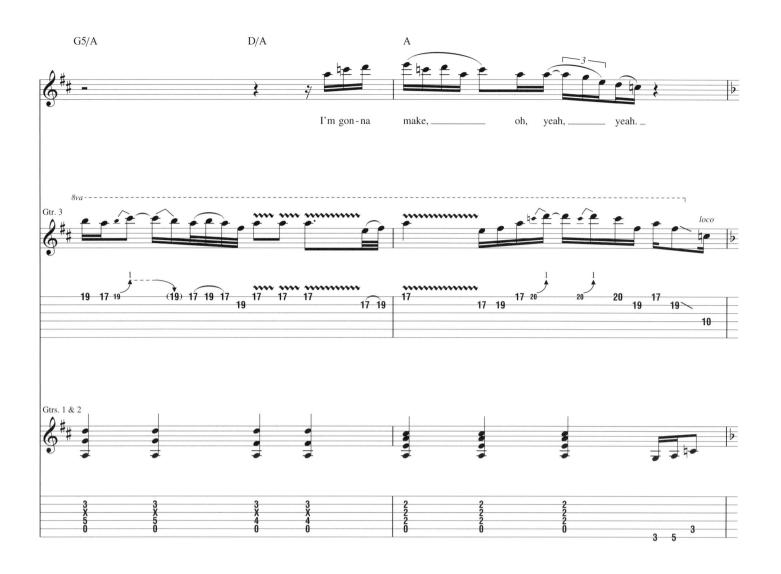

I'm gon-na   make, _____ oh, yeah, _____ yeah. __

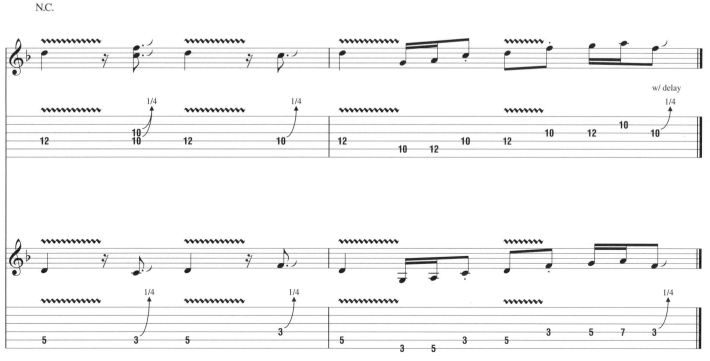

NO LOVE ON THE STREET

Words and Music by
Michael Kamen and Tim Curry

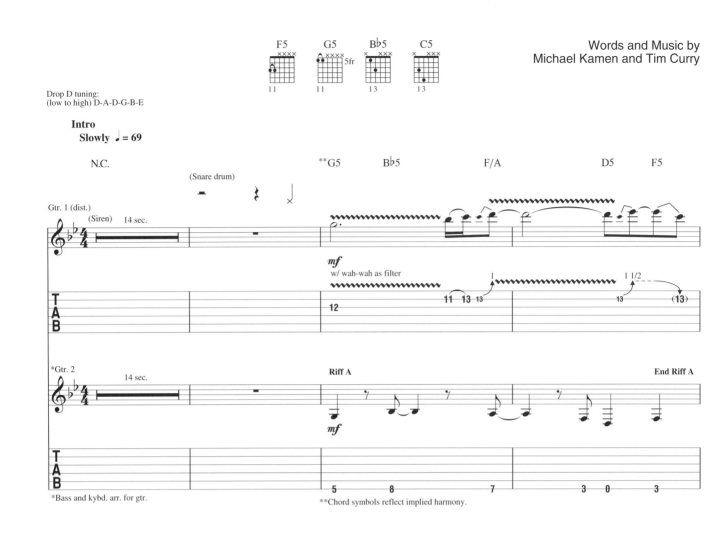

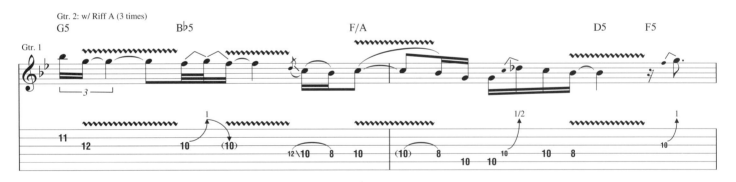

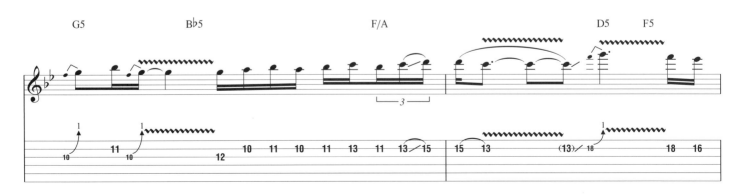

Copyright © 1979 Sony/ATV Music Publishing LLC, K-Man Corp. and Arriviste Ink Music
All Rights on behalf of Sony/ATV Music Publishing LLC and K-Man Corp.
Administered by Sony/ATV Music Publishing LLC, 8 Music Square West, Nashville, TN 37203
International Copyright Secured   All Rights Reserved

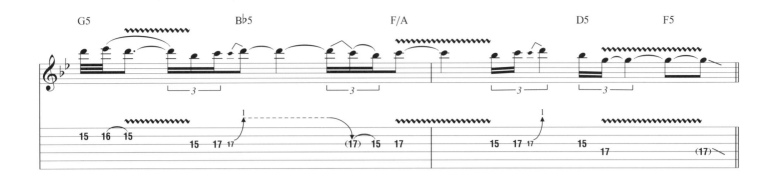

Verse

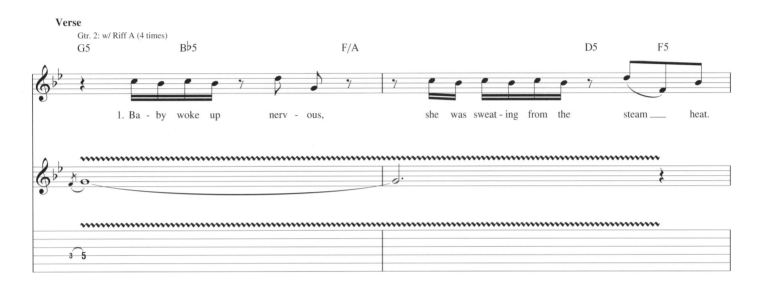

1. Ba - by woke up nerv - ous, she was sweat - ing from the steam __ heat.

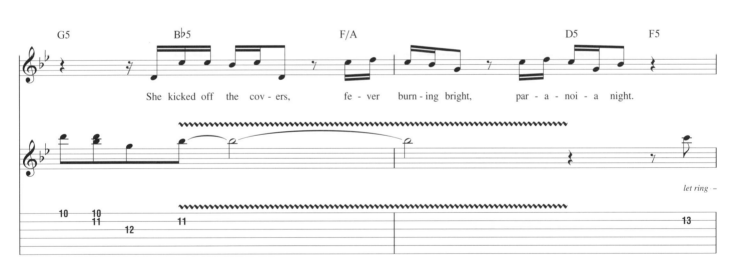

She kicked off the cov - ers, fe - ver burn - ing bright, par - a - noi - a night.

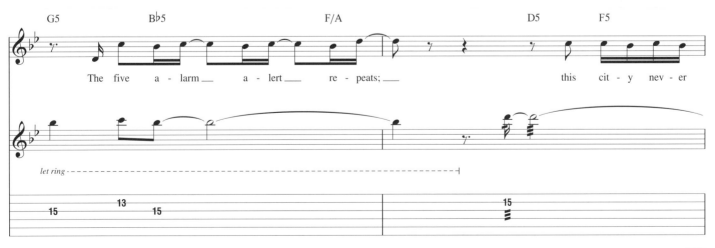

The five a - larm __ a - lert __ re - peats; __ this cit - y nev - er

Verse

Gtr. 2: w/ Riff A (4 times)

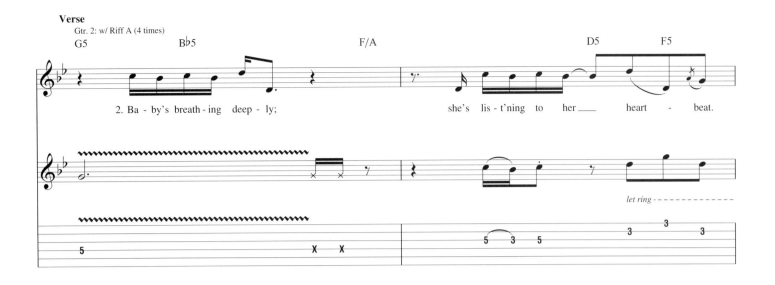

2. Ba - by's breath - ing deep - ly; she's lis - t'ning to her ___ heart - beat.

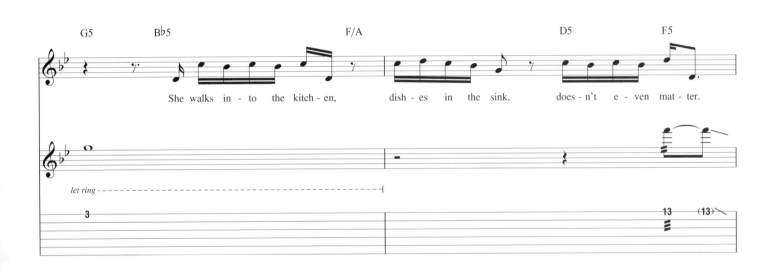

She walks in - to the kitch - en, dish - es in the sink, does - n't e - ven mat - ter.

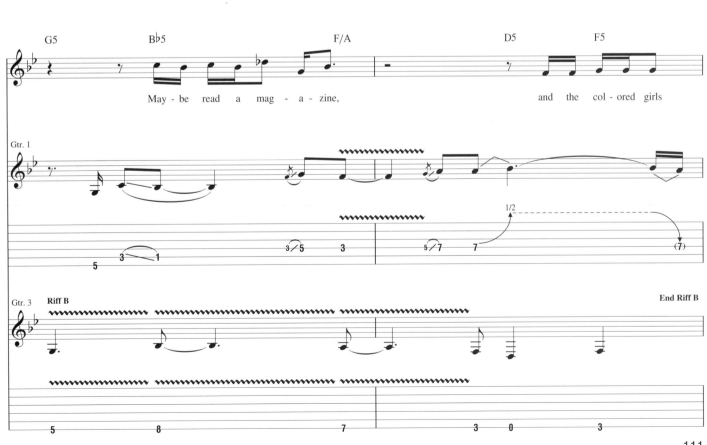

May - be read a mag - a - zine, and the col - ored girls

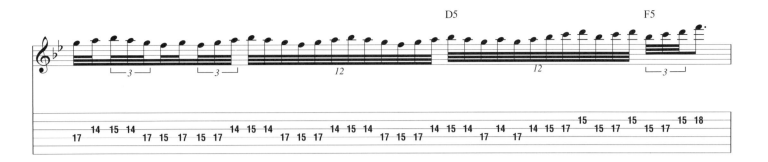

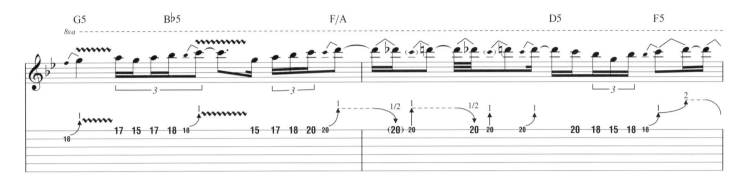

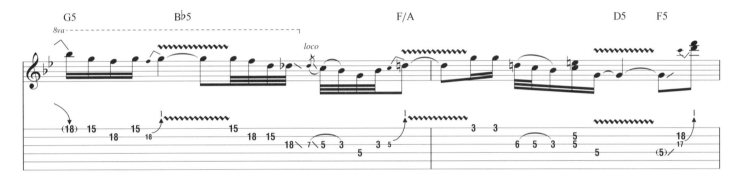

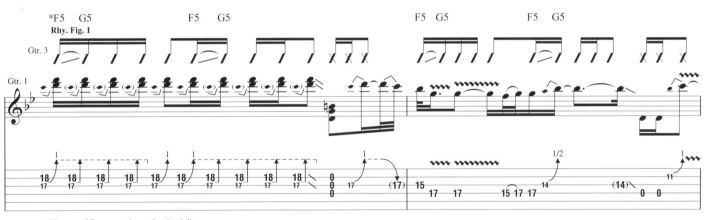

*See top of first page of song for chord diagrams
 pertaining to rhythm slashes.

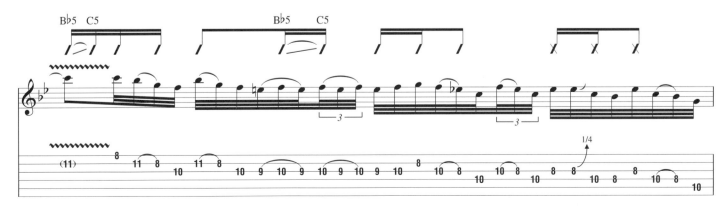

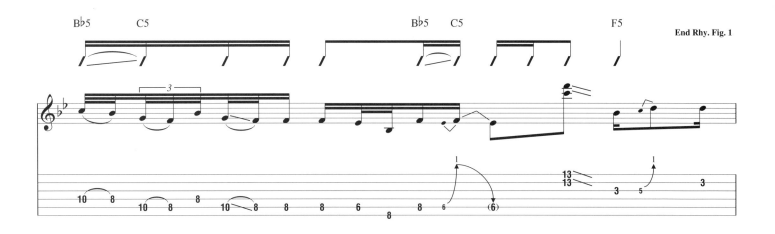

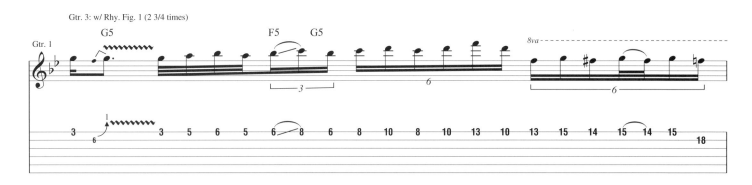

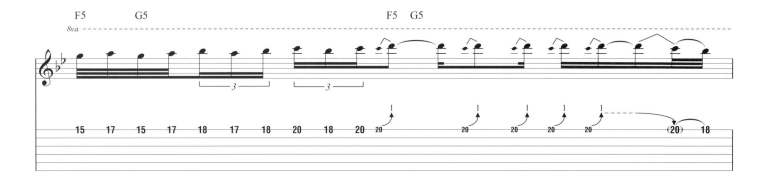

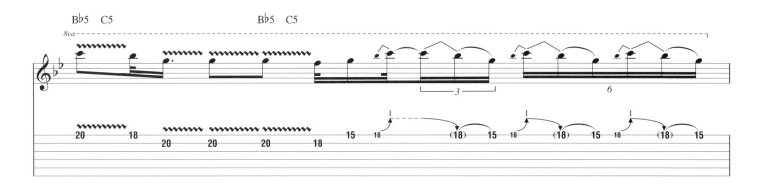

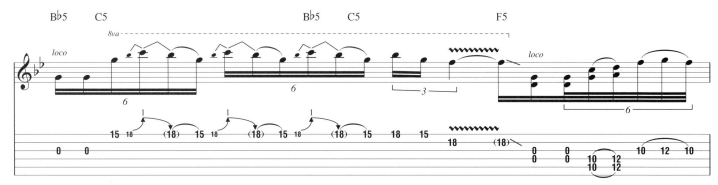

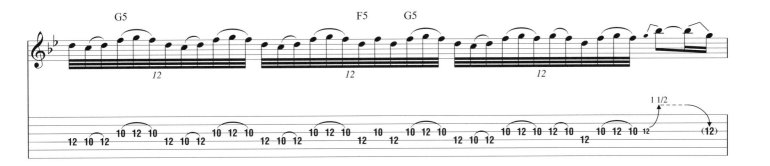

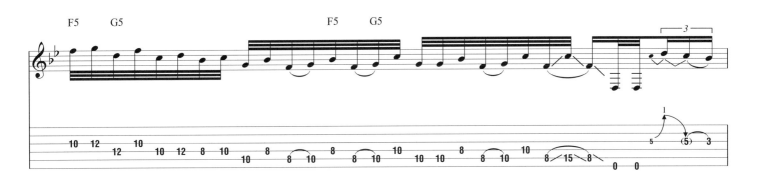

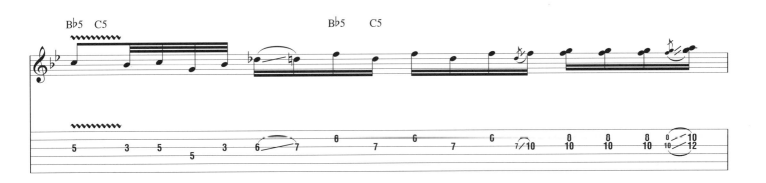

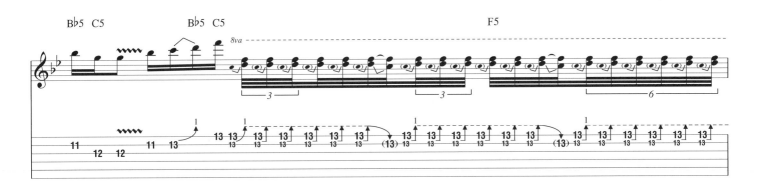

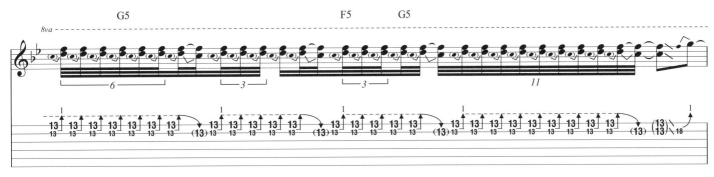

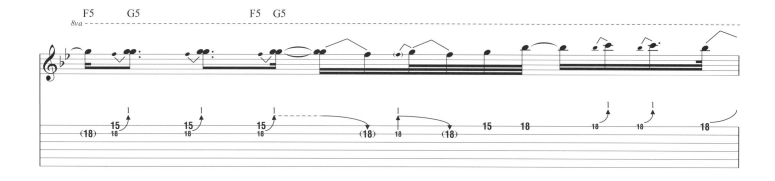

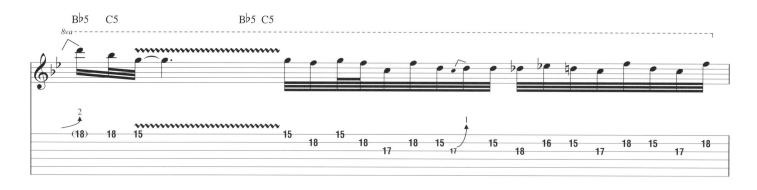

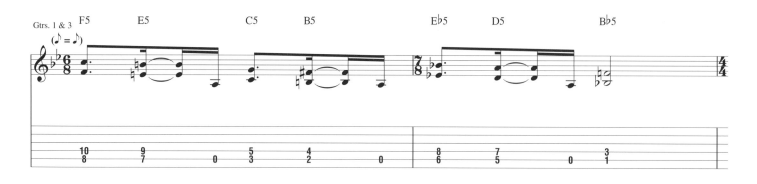

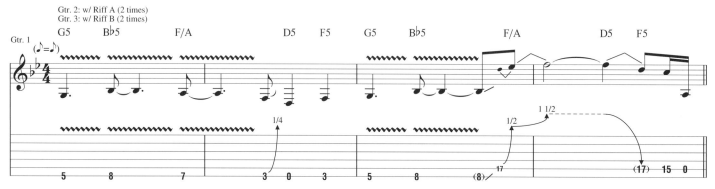

Chorus

Gtr. 3: w/ Riff C

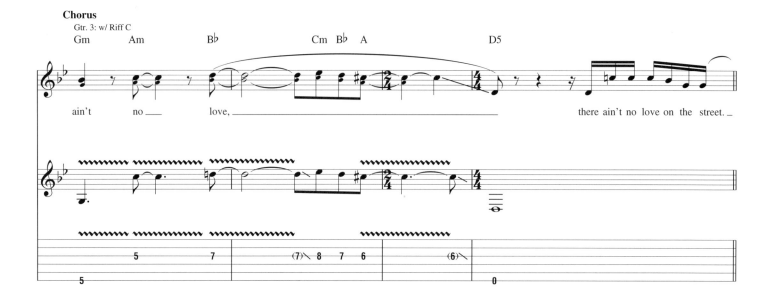

ain't   no ___ love, _____   there ain't no love on the street. _

Outro

Gtr. 2: w/ Riff A (7 times)

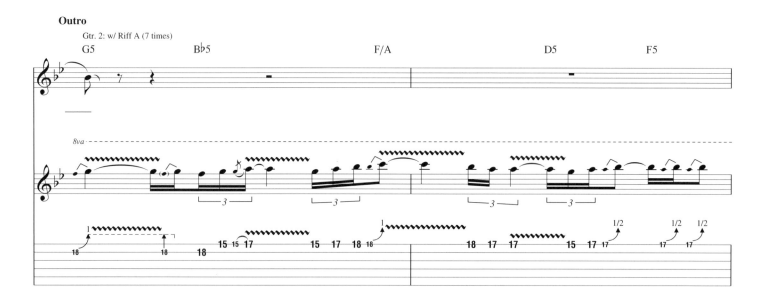

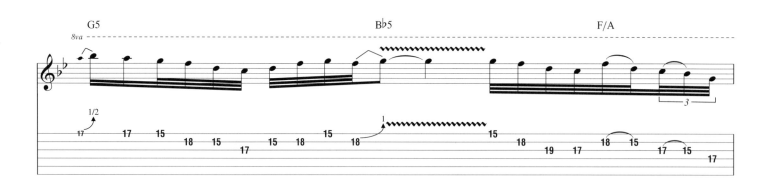

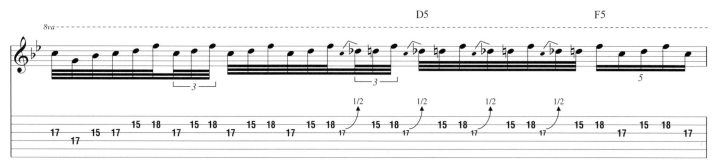

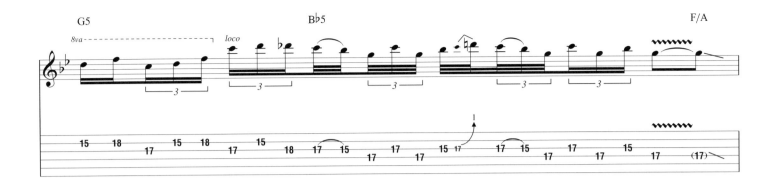

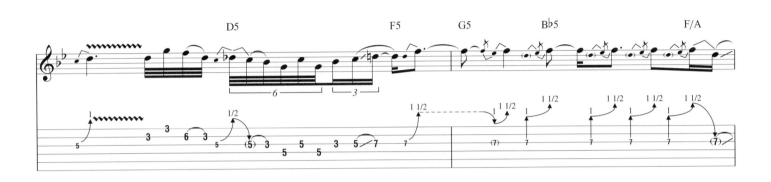

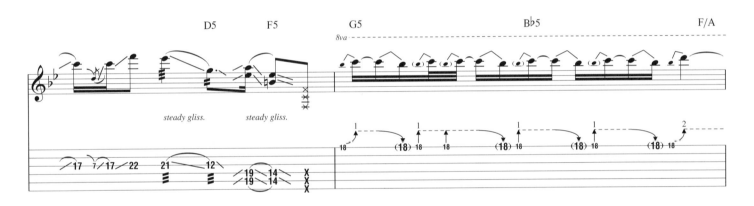

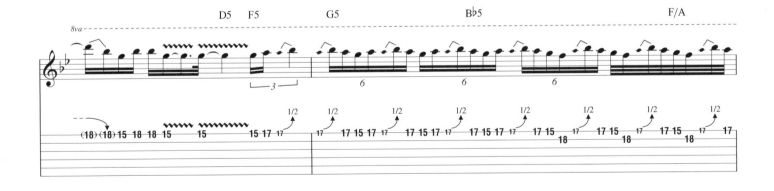

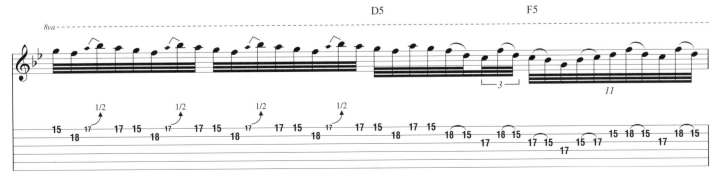

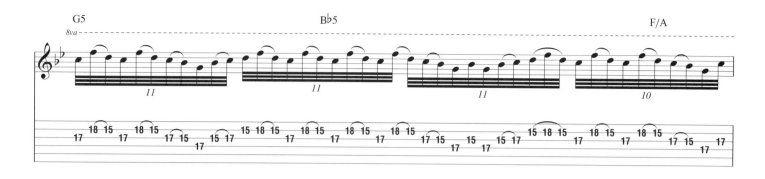

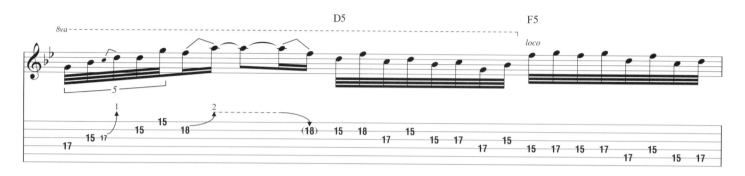

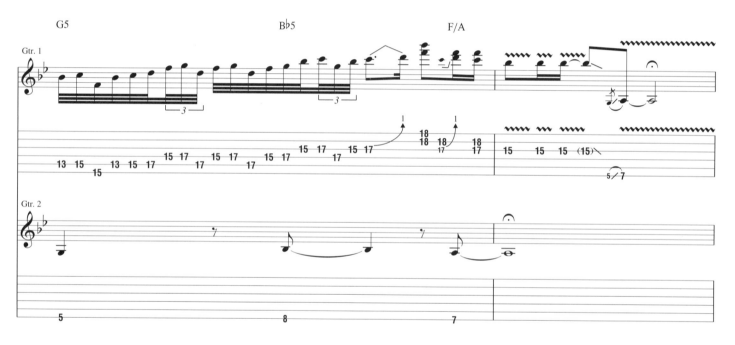

*Sound effects include fdbk., pick scrapes,
& plucking strings behind nut ad lib.

THE WHALE THAT SWALLOWED JONAH

Words and Music by
Joe Bonamassa

Copyright © 2011 Smokin' Joe Analog Music Co. (ASCAP)
International Copyright Secured   All Rights Reserved

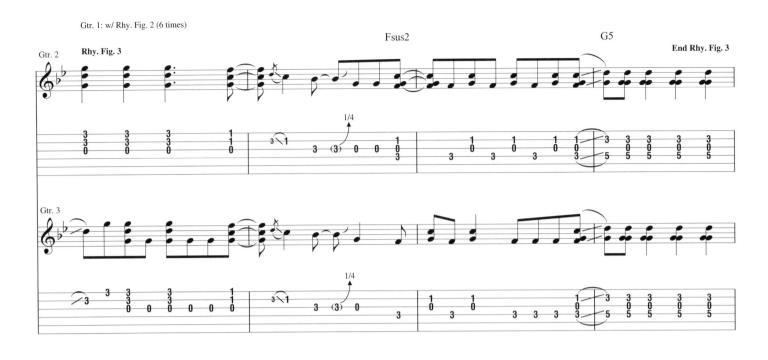

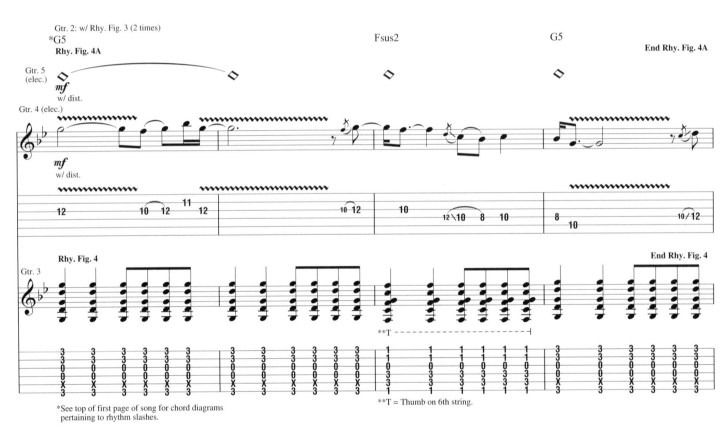

*See top of first page of song for chord diagrams pertaining to rhythm slashes.

**T = Thumb on 6th string.

1. Well, the

Verse

sun is up ___ and a-ris - ing; the wag-on's head-ed west. Now I

*Composite arrangement

Gtrs. 2 & 3: w/ Rhy. Fig. 5 (3 times)

can't ___ shake ___ that old ___ sus - pi - cion that I set-tled for sec - ond best. ___

___ I've been fru - gal at ___ my ta - ble, I've been con -

- scious, I've been blind. ___ Who ev - er said that for - ty a -

- cres and a mule ___ would ev - er keep ___ me sat - is - fied? ___

Interlude

They say the whale that swal - lowed Jo - nah out in the deep blue sea,___ some - times I ___ get that feel - ing ___ that same old whale ___ swal - lowed me. ___ They say the

125

Gtrs. 2 & 3: w/ Rhy. Fig. 4
Gtr. 5: w/ Rhy. Fig. 4A

G5   **Fsus2**   **G5**

whale that swal - lowed Jo - nah   to put me through the test, __   some - times

Gtrs. 2 & 3: w/ Rhy. Fig. 7
Gtr. 5: w/ Rhy. Fig. 7A

Fsus2   **G5**

I __ get __ that feel - ing __ that I'm dif - f'rent from the rest.

Interlude

Gtr. 1: w/ Rhy. Fig. 2 (4 times)
Gtr. 2: w/ Rhy. Fig. 3 (2 times)
Gtrs. 3 & 5: w/ Rhy. Figs. 4 & 4A (2 times)

G5   **Fsus2**   **G5**

Gtr. 4

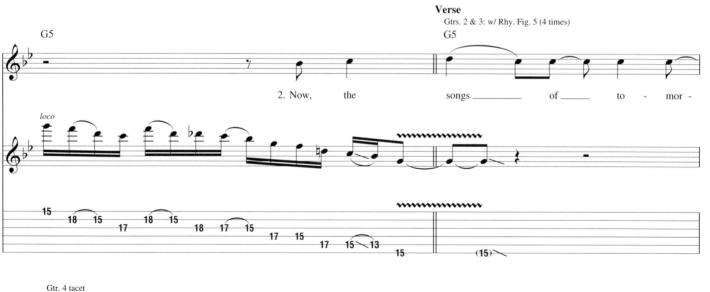

Verse
Gtrs. 2 & 3: w/ Rhy. Fig. 5 (4 times)

G5   **G5**

2. Now, the songs __ of __ to - mor -

Gtr. 4 tacet

Fsus2   **G5**

- row will come to me in time.   Life is go - ing by __ so fast __

126

now, ba - by; I have - n't had a chance to change __ my mind. __ I feel it in __ my fin -

gers; I can feel _____ it in my bones. _____ May - be it's the

whale's way __ of tell - ing me it's time to get __ your - self back home. __

Interlude

Gtrs. 2 & 5: w/ Rhy. Fig. 6
Gtr. 3: w/ Rhy. Fig. 6A

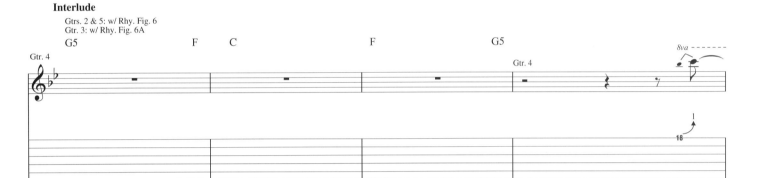

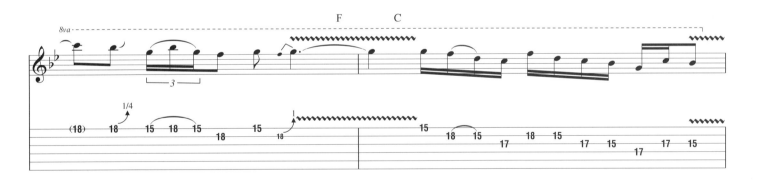

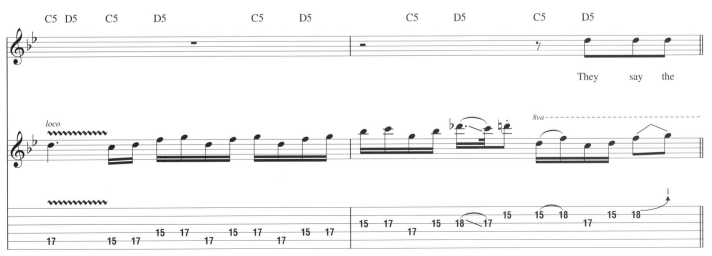

They say the

127

Chorus

Gtr. 1: w/ Rhy. Fig. 1
Gtrs. 2 & 3: w/ Rhy. Fig. 4
Gtr. 5: w/ Rhy. Fig. 4A

Gtr. 4 tacet

Gtr. 1: w/ Rhy. Fig. 2 (7 times)

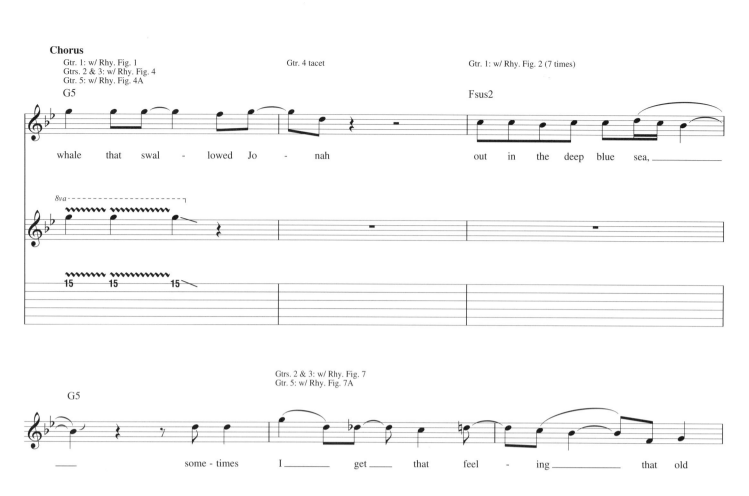

whale that swal - lowed Jo - nah ... out in the deep blue sea,

Gtrs. 2 & 3: w/ Rhy. Fig. 7
Gtr. 5: w/ Rhy. Fig. 7A

some - times I ____ get ____ that feel - ing ____ that old

Gtrs. 2 & 3: w/ Rhy. Fig. 4
Gtr. 5: w/ Rhy. Fig. 4A

whale ____ swal - lowed me. ____ They say the whale that swal - lowed Jo -

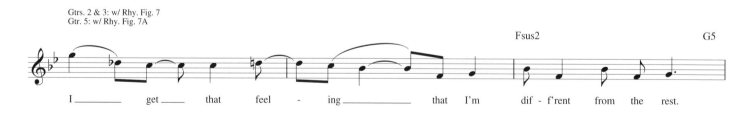

- nah to put me through the test, ____ some - times

Gtrs. 2 & 3: w/ Rhy. Fig. 7
Gtr. 5: w/ Rhy. Fig. 7A

I ____ get ____ that feel - ing ____ that I'm dif - f'rent from the rest.

Guitar Solo

Gtrs. 2 & 3: w/ Rhy. Fig. 4 (4 times)

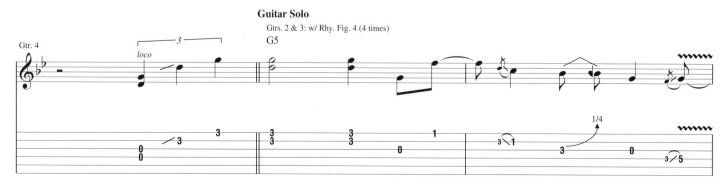

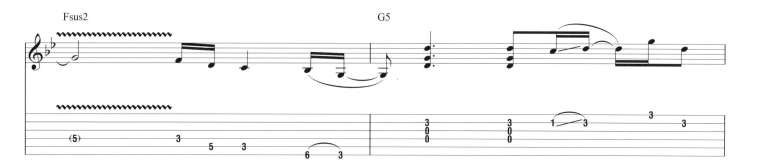

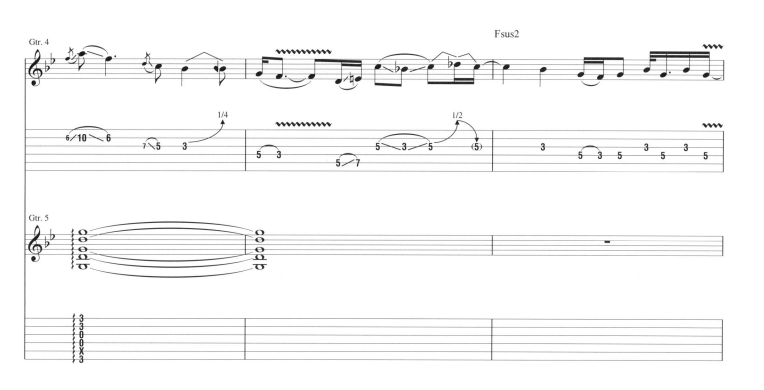

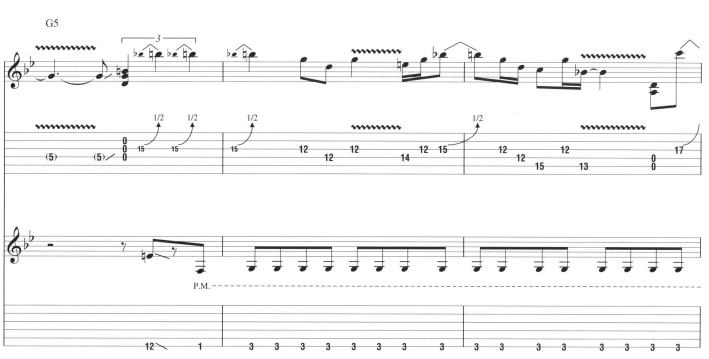

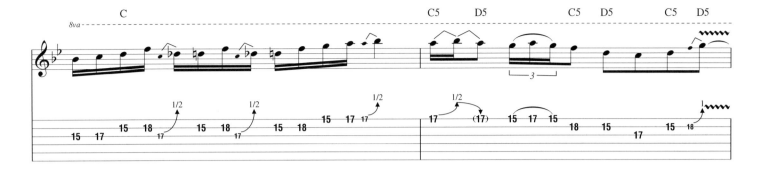

Chorus
Gtr. 1: w/ Rhy. Fig. 1
Gtrs. 2 & 3: w/ Rhy. Fig. 4
Gtr. 5: w/ Rhy. Fig. 4A

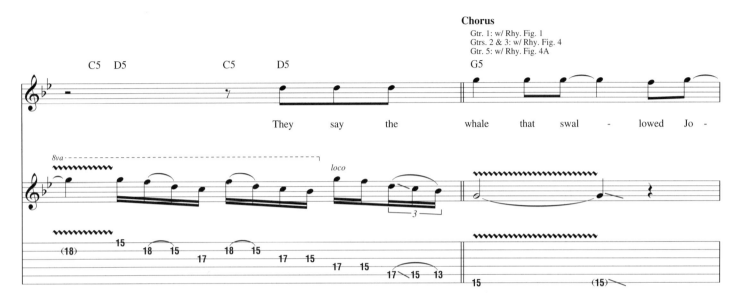

They say the whale that swal - lowed Jo -

Gtr. 4 tacet

Gtr. 1: w/ Rhy. Fig. 2 (7 times)

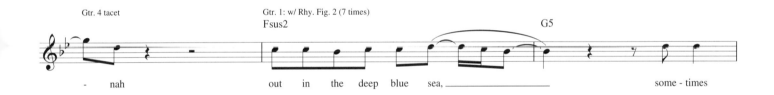

- nah out in the deep blue sea, some - times

Gtrs. 2 & 3: w/ Rhy. Fig. 7
Gtr. 5: w/ Rhy. Fig. 7A

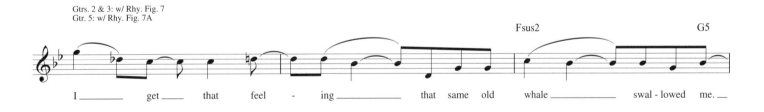

I get that feel - ing that same old whale swal - lowed me.

Gtrs. 2 & 3: w/ Rhy. Fig. 4
Gtr. 5: w/ Rhy. Fig. 4A

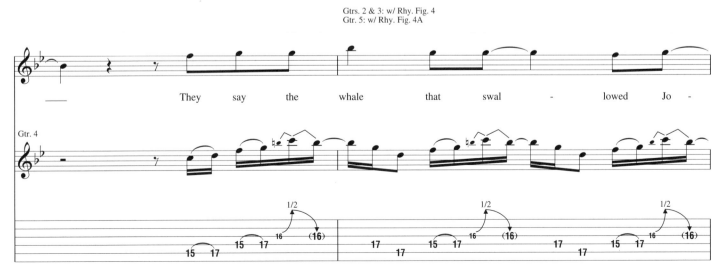

They say the whale that swal - lowed Jo -

Gtr. 4

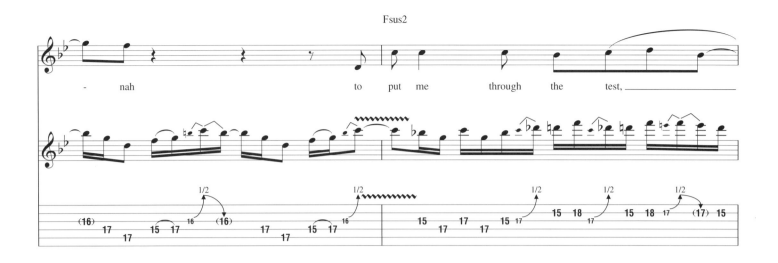

to put me through the test, _____

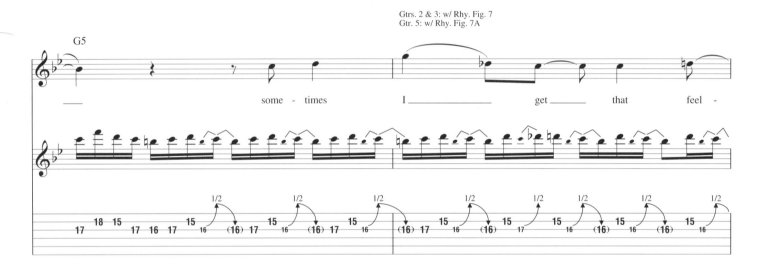

some-times I _____ get _____ that feel-

-ing _____ that I'm dif-f'rent from the rest.

Outro

Gtr. 1: w/ Rhy. Fig. 1 (3 1/2 times)
Gtr. 2: w/ Rhy. Fig. 3 (1 3/4 times)
Gtrs. 3 & 5: w/ Rhy. Figs. 4 & 4A (1 3/4 times)

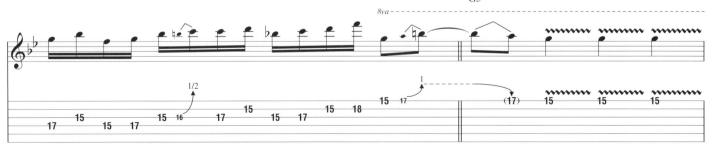

Fsus2

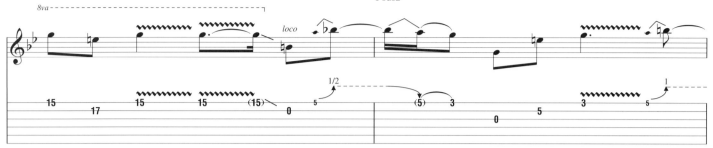

G5

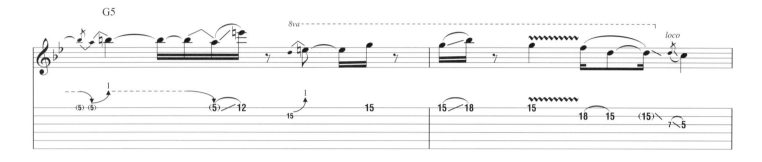

Fsus2

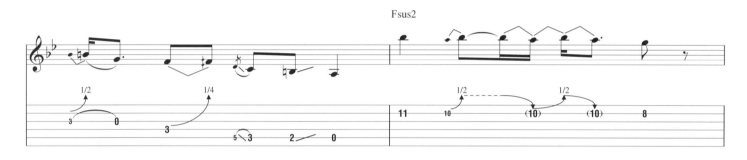

Free time

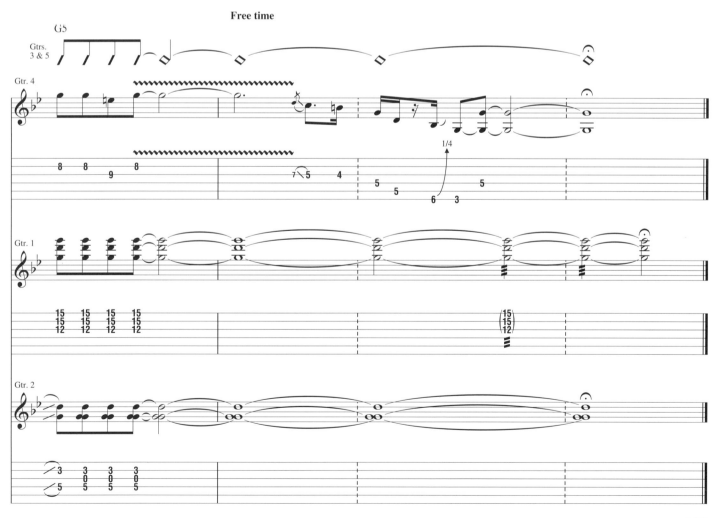

133

SWEET ROWENA

Words and Music by
Vince Gill and Pete Wasner

*Chord symbols reflect basic harmony.

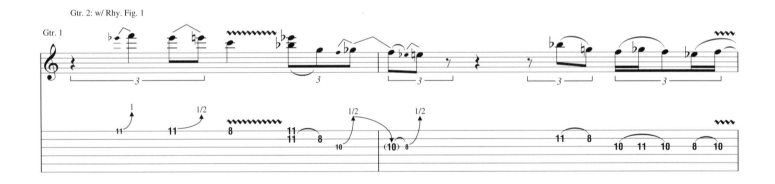

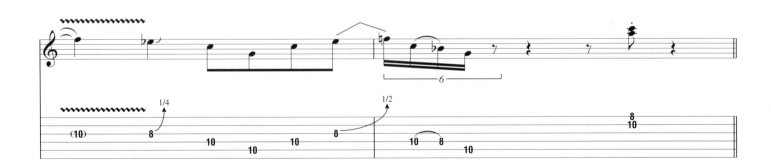

Copyright © 2010 VINNY MAE MUSIC and UNCLE PETE MUSIC
All Rights Reserved   Used by Permission

Verse

C7

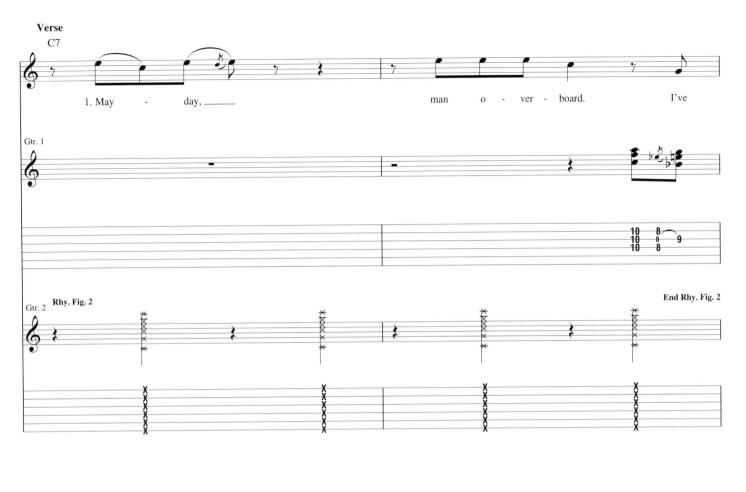

1. May - day, _____ man o - ver - board. I've

Gtr. 1

Gtr. 2

Rhy. Fig. 2   **End Rhy. Fig. 2**

Gtr. 2: w/ Rhy. Fig. 2 (3 times)

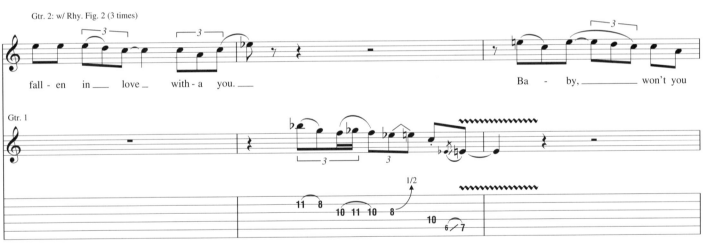

fall - en in ___ love ___ with - a you. ___   Ba - by, _____ won't you

Gtr. 1

1/2

save ___ me, _____ 'cause with - out you I just won't pull through. _____   Uh, sweet Ro -

*T

*T = Thumb on 6th string.

135

Chorus

we - na, won't you call my num - ber?____ Uh, sweet Ro - we - na, won't you call ____ my name?____

____ Throw me a line; I'm ____ go - ing un - der ____ and my

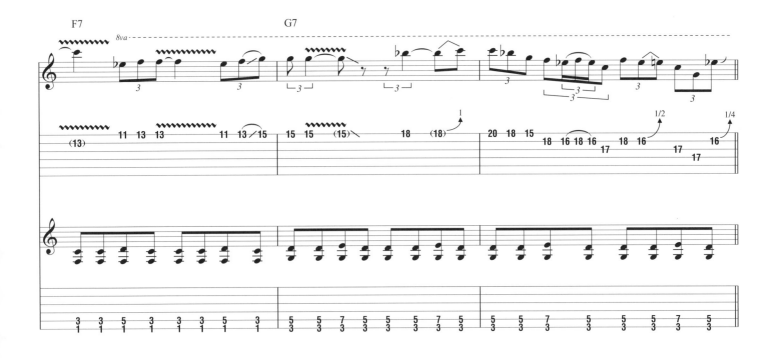

Verse

Gtr. 2: w/ Rhy. Fig. 2 (4 times)

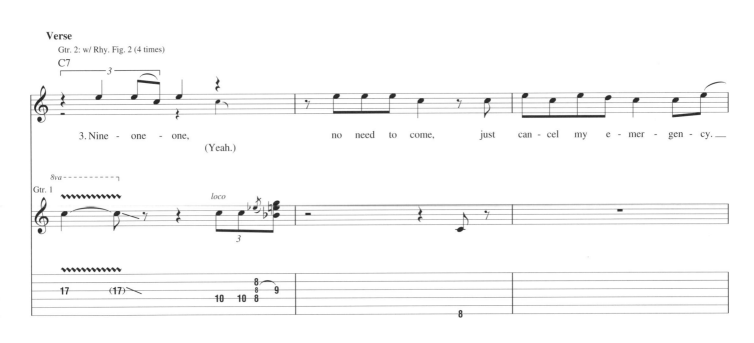

3. Nine - one - one, (Yeah.) no need to come, just can - cel my e - mer - gen - cy.

(Oh, my e - mer-gen-cy, ba - by.) The sweet-est thing, ___ Lord, I've ___ ev - er seen ___ is

Outro-Guitar Solo

Gtr. 2: w/ Rhy. Fig. 4 (11 times)

143

Love Theme from "The Eyes of Laura Mars"

PRISONER

from THE EYES OF LAURA MARS

Words and Music by
Karen Lawrence and John Desautels

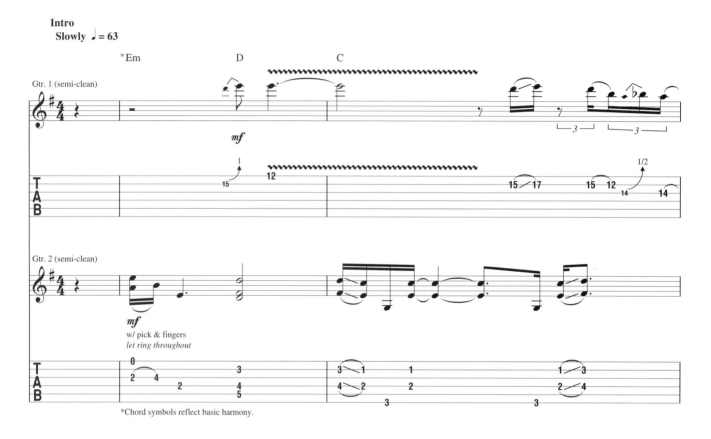

*Chord symbols reflect basic harmony.

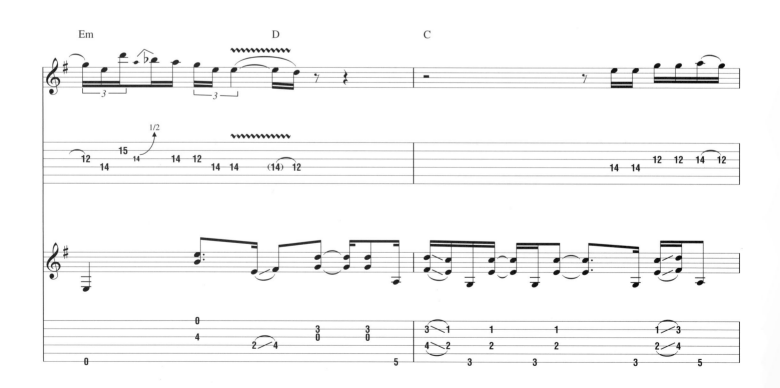

© 1977 (Renewed 2005), 1978 EMI SOSAHA MUSIC INC., JONATHAN THREE MUSIC and DIANA MUSIC CORP.
All Rights Reserved   International Copyright Secured   Used by Permission

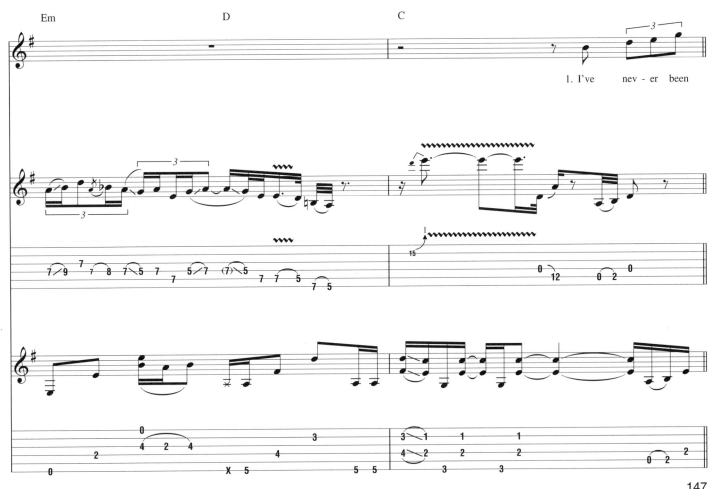

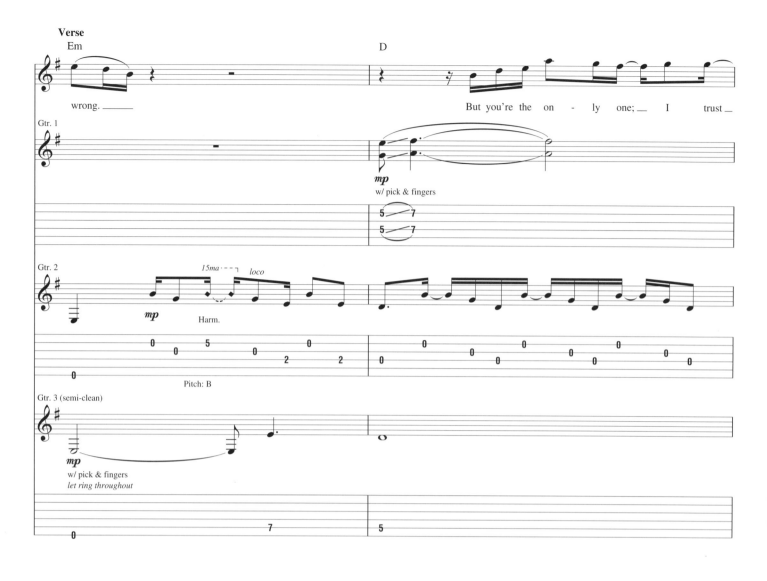

Pre-Chorus

What __ is __ it a - bout __ you? __

Some kind of light __ shines __ from your face, __

'cause I____ can't turn a-way.____

I'm like a

Chorus

pris - on - er,

cap - tured in ____ your eyes. ____

I've been

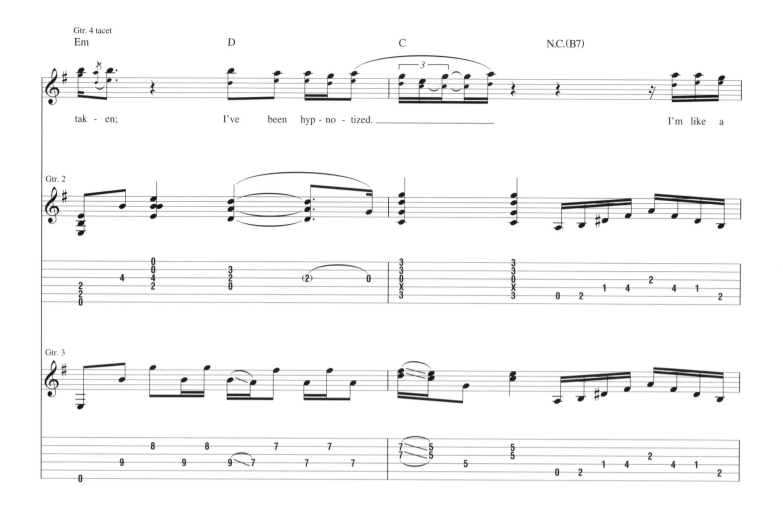

tak - en; I've been hyp - no - tized. _____ I'm like a

pris - on - er, cap - tured in ___ your eyes. _____ Oh, I've been

ev - er. ____ Well, I can't es - cape. ____ One min - ute so __

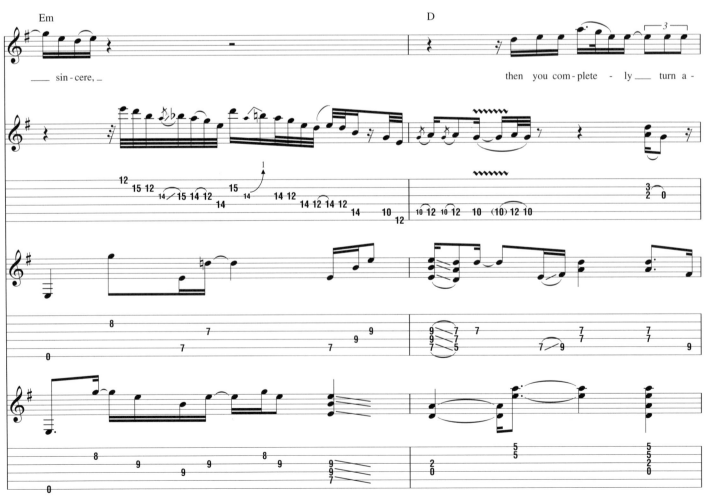

____ sin - cere, __ then you com - plete - ly __ turn a -

'cause if you want _____ me at night I'll stay, _____

and I _____ can't turn a - way. _____

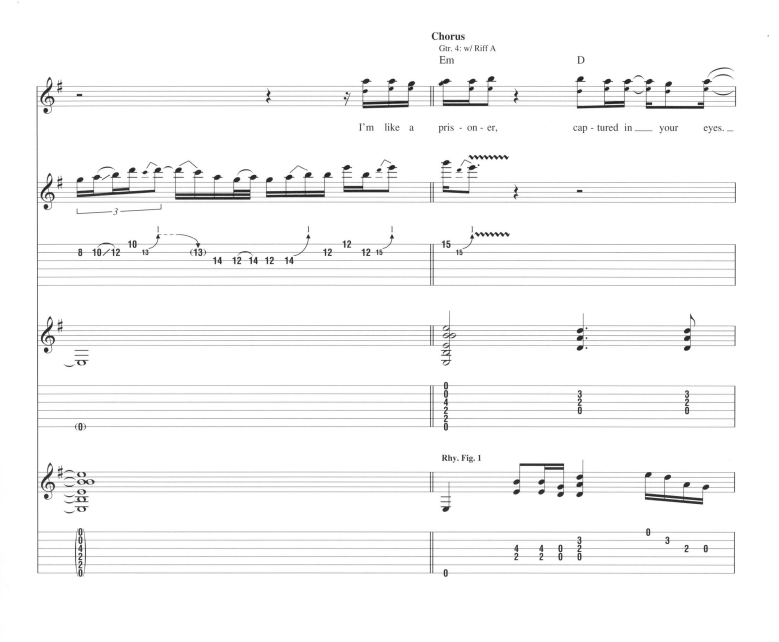

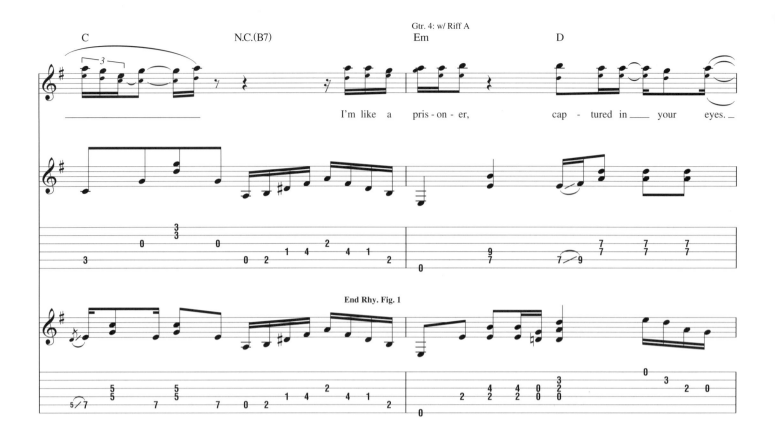

I'm like a pris - on - er,   cap - tured in ___ your   eyes. ___

Oh, I've been tak - en; ____   I've   been hyp - no - tized, ____

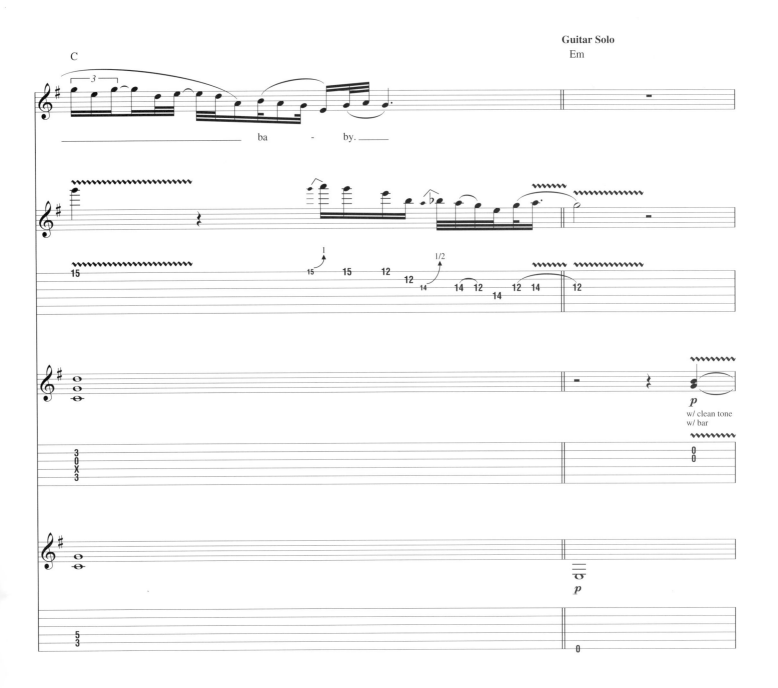

ba - by. _____

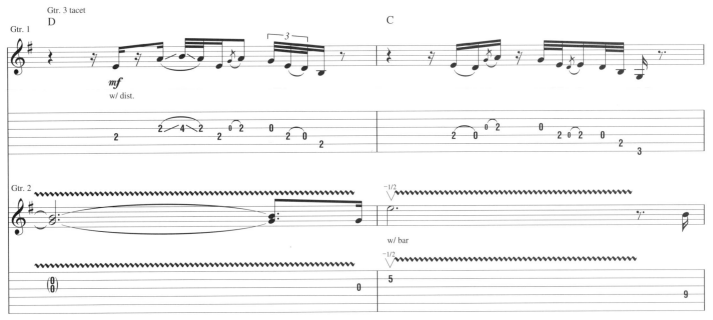

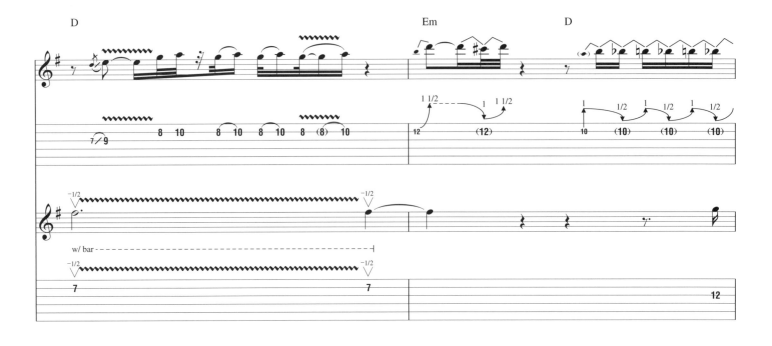

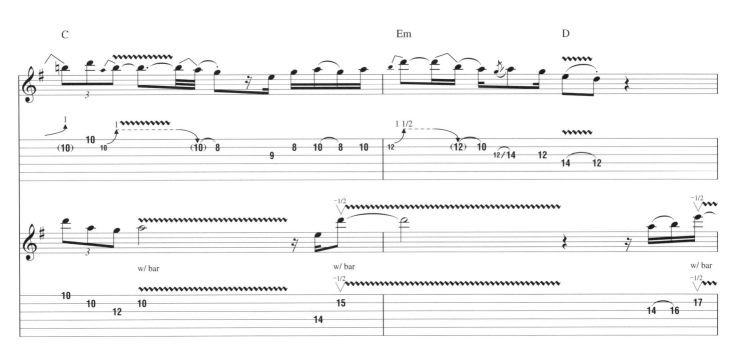

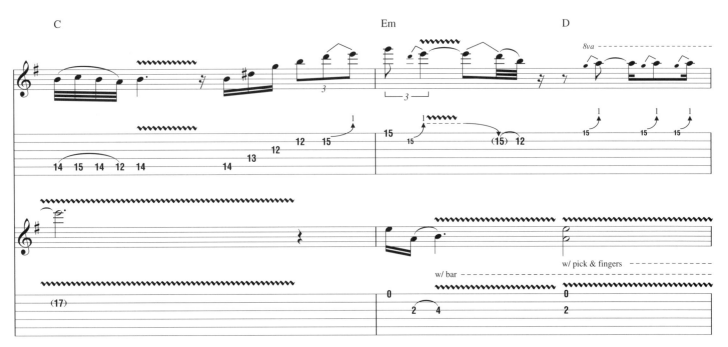

162

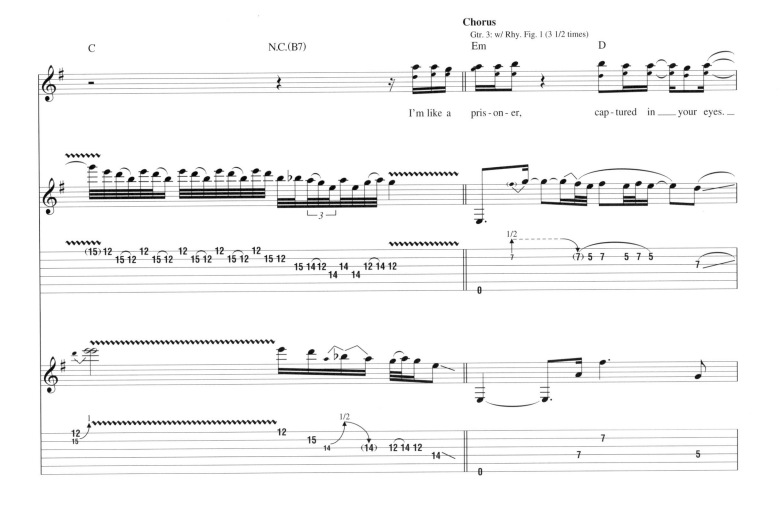

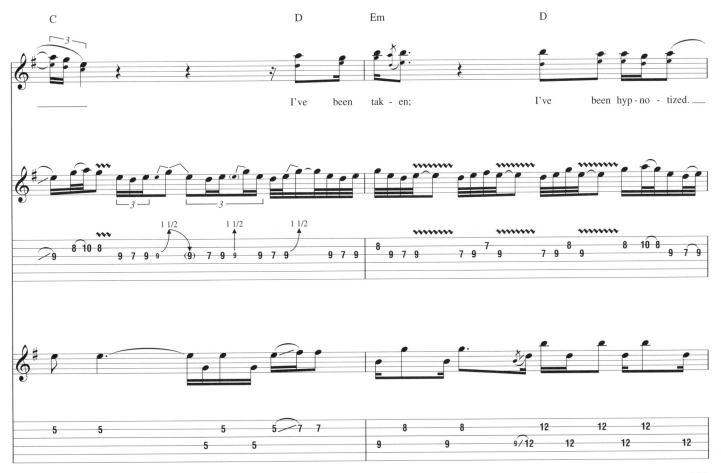

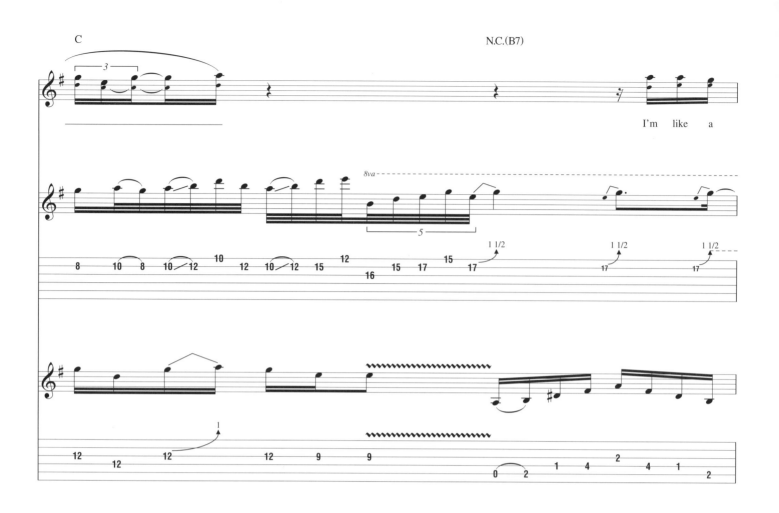

C   N.C.(B7)

I'm   like   a

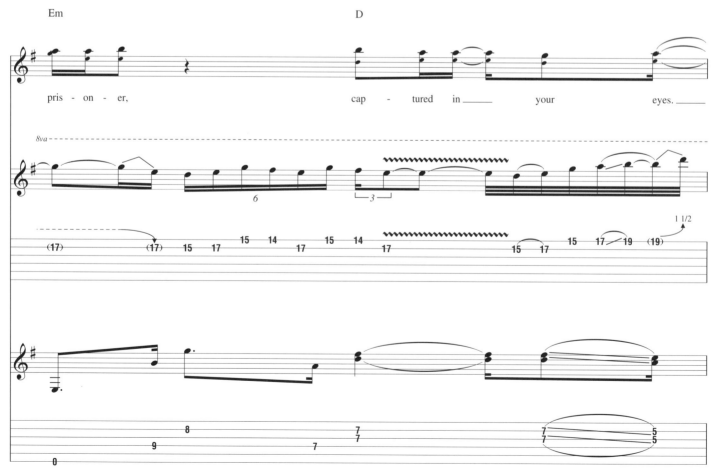

Em   D

pris - on - er,   cap - tured in _____ your   eyes. _____

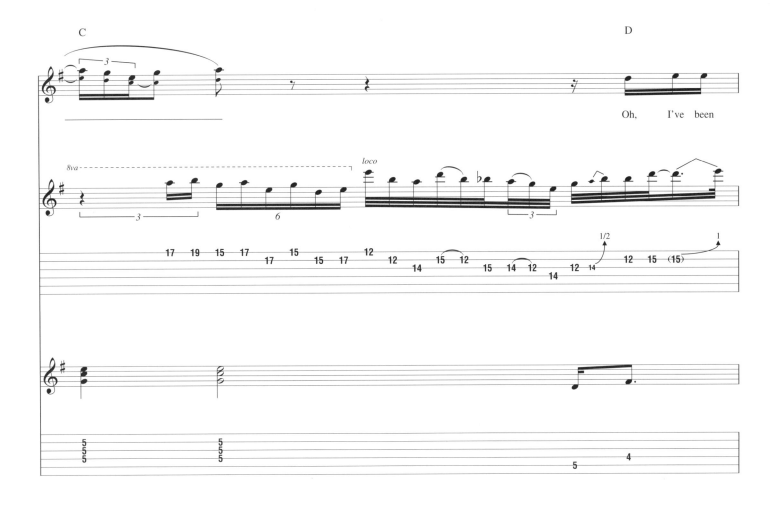

Oh, I've been

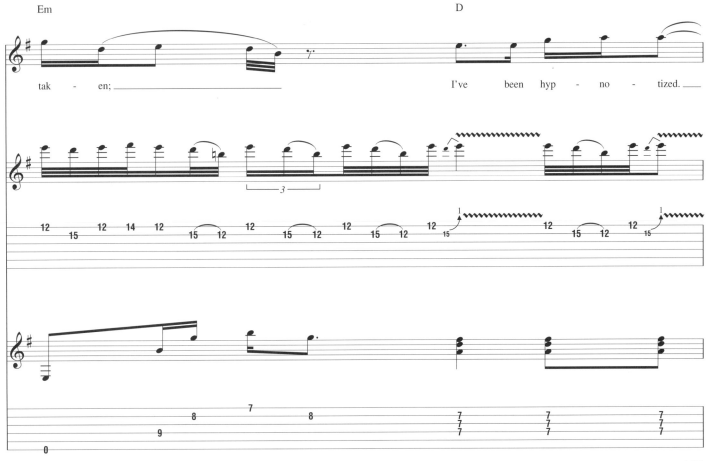

tak - en; _____ I've been hyp - no - tized. _____

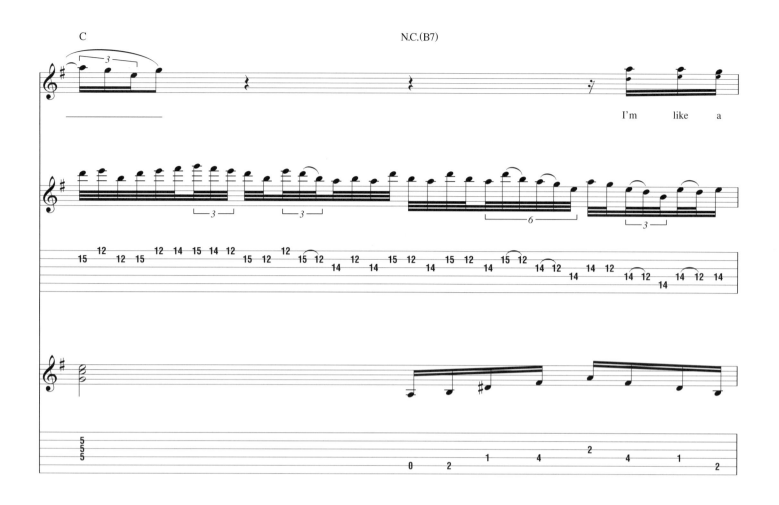

I'm   like   a

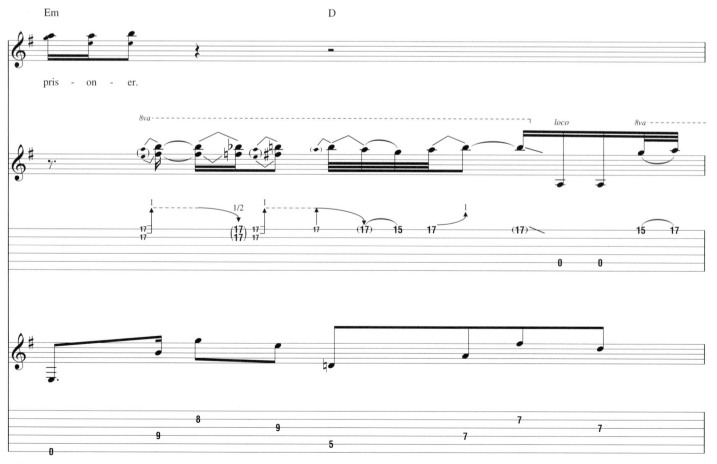

pris - on - er.

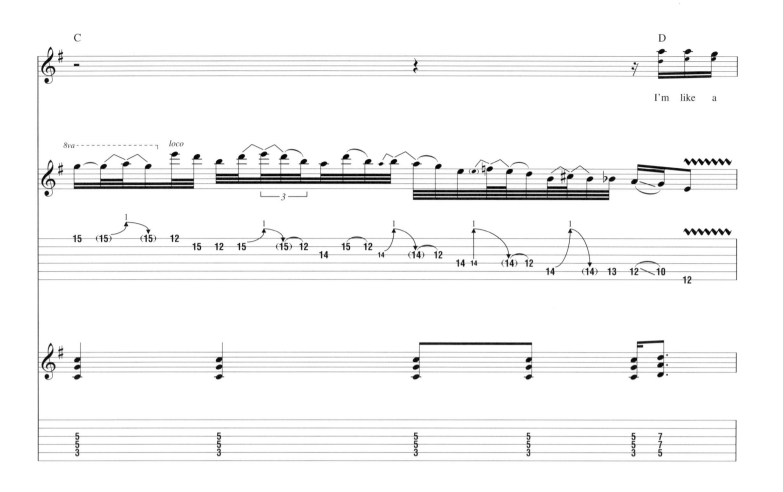

I'm like a

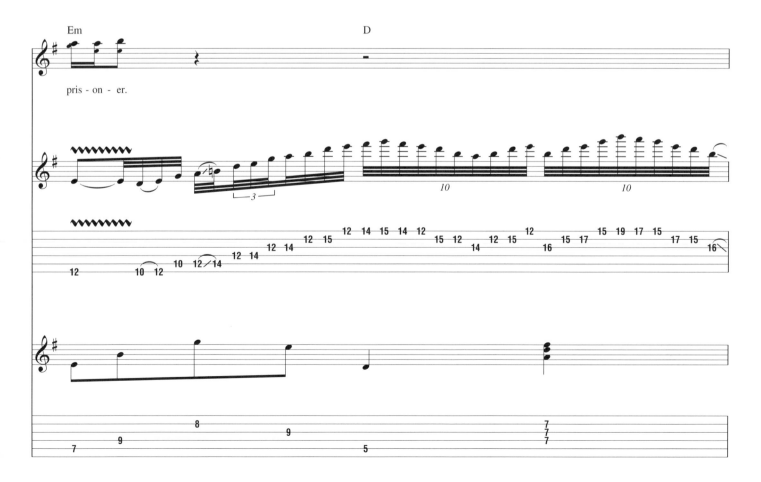

pris - on - er.

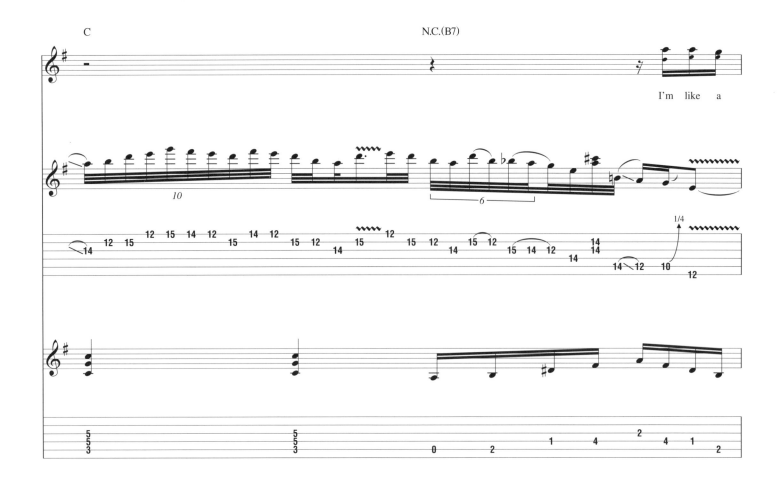

I'm like a

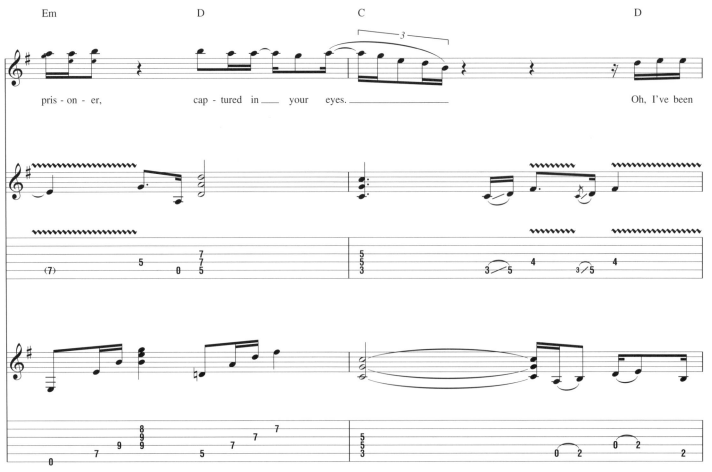

pris - on - er,   cap - tured in ___ your eyes. _____   Oh, I've been

tak - en; _____ I've been hyp - no - tized, _____ ba - by. _____

Outro

*Vol. swells

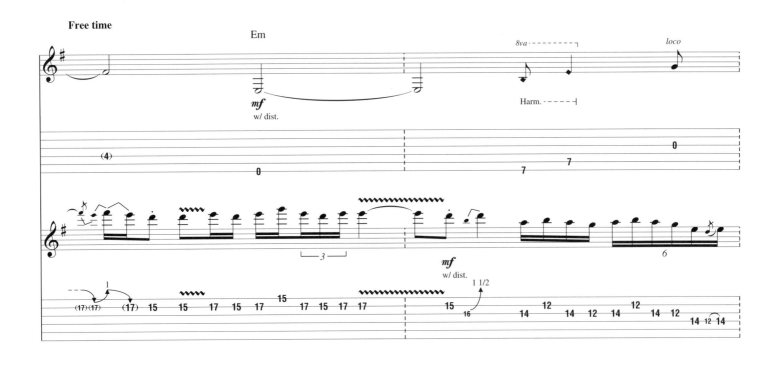

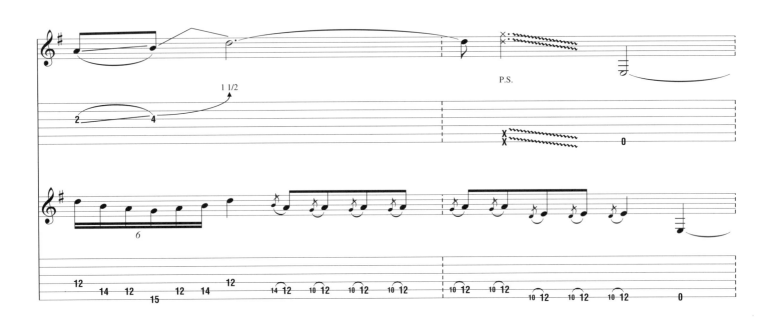

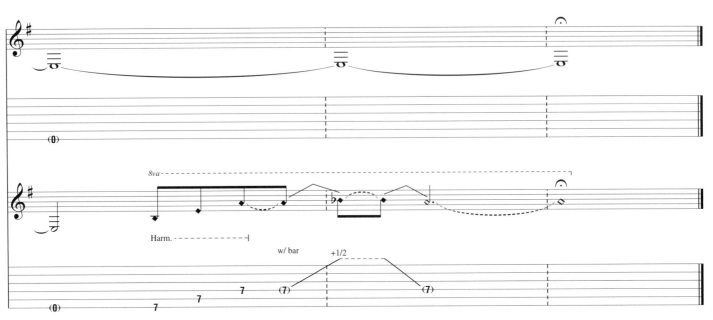

GUITAR NOTATION LEGEND

Guitar music can be notated three different ways: on a *musical staff*, in *tablature*, and in *rhythm slashes*.

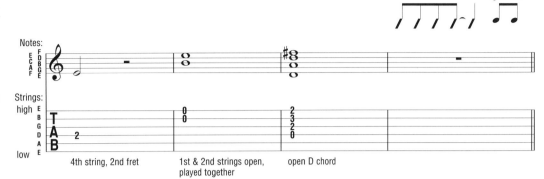

RHYTHM SLASHES are written above the staff. Strum chords in the rhythm indicated. Use the chord diagrams found at the top of the first page of the transcription for the appropriate chord voicings. Round noteheads indicate single notes.

THE MUSICAL STAFF shows pitches and rhythms and is divided by bar lines into measures. Pitches are named after the first seven letters of the alphabet.

TABLATURE graphically represents the guitar fingerboard. Each horizontal line represents a string, and each number represents a fret.

HALF-STEP BEND: Strike the note and bend up 1/2 step.

BEND AND RELEASE: Strike the note and bend up as indicated, then release back to the original note. Only the first note is struck.

HAMMER-ON: Strike the first (lower) note with one finger, then sound the higher note (on the same string) with another finger by fretting it without picking.

TRILL: Very rapidly alternate between the notes indicated by continuously hammering on and pulling off.

PICK SCRAPE: The edge of the pick is rubbed down (or up) the string, producing a scratchy sound.

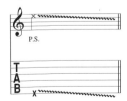

TREMOLO PICKING: The note is picked as rapidly and continuously as possible.

WHOLE-STEP BEND: Strike the note and bend up one step.

PRE-BEND: Bend the note as indicated, then strike it.

PULL-OFF: Place both fingers on the notes to be sounded. Strike the first note and without picking, pull the finger off to sound the second (lower) note.

TAPPING: Hammer ("tap") the fret indicated with the pick-hand index or middle finger and pull off to the note fretted by the fret hand.

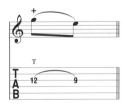

MUFFLED STRINGS: A percussive sound is produced by laying the fret hand across the string(s) without depressing, and striking them with the pick hand.

VIBRATO BAR DIVE AND RETURN: The pitch of the note or chord is dropped a specified number of steps (in rhythm), then returned to the original pitch.

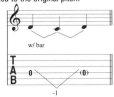

GRACE NOTE BEND: Strike the note and immediately bend up as indicated.

VIBRATO: The string is vibrated by rapidly bending and releasing the note with the fretting hand.

LEGATO SLIDE: Strike the first note and then slide the same fret-hand finger up or down to the second note. The second note is not struck.

NATURAL HARMONIC: Strike the note while the fret-hand lightly touches the string directly over the fret indicated.

PALM MUTING: The note is partially muted by the pick hand lightly touching the string(s) just before the bridge.

VIBRATO BAR SCOOP: Depress the bar just before striking the note, then quickly release the bar.

SLIGHT (MICROTONE) BEND: Strike the note and bend up 1/4 step.

WIDE VIBRATO: The pitch is varied to a greater degree by vibrating with the fretting hand.

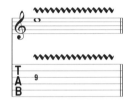

SHIFT SLIDE: Same as legato slide, except the second note is struck.

PINCH HARMONIC: The note is fretted normally and a harmonic is produced by adding the edge of the thumb or the tip of the index finger of the pick hand to the normal pick attack.

RAKE: Drag the pick across the strings indicated with a single motion.

VIBRATO BAR DIP: Strike the note and then immediately drop a specified number of steps, then release back to the original pitch.

THE HOTTEST TAB SONGBOOKS AVAILABLE FOR GUITAR & BASS!

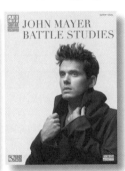

from

Guitar Transcriptions

02501410	The Black Keys – Attack & Release	$19.99
02501500	The Black Keys – A Collection	$19.99
02500702	Best of Black Label Society	$22.95
02500842	Black Label Society – Mafia	$19.95
02500116	Black Sabbath – Riff by Riff	$14.95
02500882	Blues Masters by the Bar	$19.95
02500921	Best of Joe Bonamassa	$22.95
02501510	Joe Bonamassa Collection	$24.99
02501272	Bush – 16 Stone	$21.95
02500179	Mary Chapin Carpenter Authentic Guitar Style of	$16.95
02500336	Eric Clapton – Just the Riffs	$12.99
02501565	Coheed and Cambria – Year of the Black Rainbow	$19.99
02501439	David Cook	$22.99
02500684	Dashboard Confessional – A Mark • A Mission • A Brand • A Scar	$19.95
02500689	Dashboard Confessional – The Places You Have Come to Fear the Most	$17.95
02500843	Dashboard Confessional – The Swiss Army Romance	$17.95
02501481	Brett Dennen – So Much More	$19.99
02506878	John Denver Anthology for Easy Guitar Revised Edition	$15.95
02506901	John Denver Authentic Guitar Style	$14.95
02500984	John Denver – Folk Singer	$19.95
02506928	John Denver – Greatest Hits for Fingerstyle Guitar	$14.95
02500632	John Denver Collection Strum & Sing Series	$9.95
02501448	Best of Ronnie James Dio	$22.99
02500607	The Best of Dispatch	$19.95
02500198	Best of Foreigner	$19.95
02500990	Donavon Frankenreiter	$19.95
02501242	Guns N' Roses – Anthology	$24.95
02506953	Guns N' Roses – Appetite for Destruction	$22.95
02501286	Guns N' Roses Complete, Volume 1	$24.95
02501287	Guns N' Roses Complete, Volume 2	$24.95
02506211	Guns N' Roses – 5 of the Best, Vol. 1	$12.95
02506975	Guns N' Roses – GN'R Lies	$19.95
02500299	Guns N' Roses – Live Era '87-'93 Highlights	$24.95
02501193	Guns N' Roses – Use Your Illusion I	$24.99
02501194	Guns N' Roses – Use Your Illusion II	$24.95
02506325	Metallica – The Art of Kirk Hammett	$17.95
02500939	Hawthorne Heights – The Silence in Black and White	$19.95
02500458	Best of Warren Haynes	$22.95
02500476	Warren Haynes – Guide to Slide Guitar	$17.95

02500387	Best of Heart	$19.95
02500016	The Art of James Hetfield	$17.95
02500873	Jazz for the Blues Guitarist	$14.95
02500554	Jack Johnson – Brushfire Fairytales	$19.95
02500831	Jack Johnson – In Between Dreams	$19.95
02500653	Jack Johnson – On and On	$19.95
02501139	Jack Johnson – Sleep Through the Static	$19.95
02500858	Jack Johnson – Strum & Sing	$14.99
02501564	Jack Johnson – To the Sea	$19.99
02500380	Lenny Kravitz – Greatest Hits	$19.95
02500024	Best of Lenny Kravitz	$19.95
02500129	Adrian Legg – Pickin' 'n' Squintin'	$19.95
02500362	Best of Little Feat	$19.95
02501094	Hooks That Kill – The Best of Mick Mars & Mötley Crüe	$19.95
02500305	Best of The Marshall Tucker Band	$19.95
02501077	Dave Matthews Band – Anthology	$24.99
02501357	Dave Matthews Band – Before These Crowded Streets	$19.95
02501279	Dave Matthews Band – Crash	$19.95
02501266	Dave Matthews Band – Under the Table and Dreaming	$19.95
02500131	Dave Matthews/Tim Reynolds – Live at Luther College, Vol. 1	$19.95
02500611	Dave Matthews/Tim Reynolds – Live at Luther College, Vol. 2	$22.95
02501502	John Mayer – Battle Studies	$22.99
02500986	John Mayer – Continuum	$22.99
02500705	John Mayer – Heavier Things	$22.95
02500705	John Mayer – Heavier Things	$22.95
02500529	John Mayer – Room for Squares	$22.95
02506965	Metallica – ...And Justice for All	$22.99
02501267	Metallica – Death Magnetic	$24.95
02506210	Metallica – 5 of the Best/Vol.1	$12.95
02506235	Metallica – 5 of the Best/Vol. 2	$12.95
02500070	Metallica – Garage, Inc.	$24.95
02507018	Metallica – Kill 'Em All	$19.99
02501232	Metallica – Live: Binge & Purge	$19.95
02501275	Metallica – Load	$24.95
02507920	Metallica – Master of Puppets	$19.95
02501195	Metallica – Metallica	$22.95
02501297	Metallica – ReLoad	$24.95
02507019	Metallica – Ride the Lightning	$19.95
02500279	Metallica – S&M Highlights	$24.95
02500638	Metallica – St. Anger	$24.95
02500577	Molly Hatchet – 5 of the Best	$9.95
02501529	Monte Montgomery Collection	$24.99
02500846	Best of Steve Morse Band and Dixie Dregs	$19.95

02500765	Jason Mraz – Waiting for My Rocket to Come	$19.95
02501324	Jason Mraz – We Sing, We Dance, We Steal Things.	$22.99
02500448	Best of Ted Nugent	$19.95
02500707	Ted Nugent – Legendary Licks	$19.95
02500844	Best of O.A.R. (Of a Revolution)	$22.95
02500348	Ozzy Osbourne – Blizzard of Ozz	$19.95
02501277	Ozzy Osbourne – Diary of a Madman	$19.95
02507904	Ozzy Osbourne/Randy Rhoads Tribute	$22.95
02500524	The Bands of Ozzfest	$16.95
02500680	Don't Stop Believin': The Steve Perry Anthology	$22.95
02500025	Primus Anthology – A-N (Guitar/Bass)	$19.95
02500091	Primus Anthology – O-Z (Guitar/Bass)	$19.95
02500468	Primus – Sailing the Seas of Cheese	$19.95
02500875	Queens of the Stone Age – Lullabies to Paralyze	$24.95
02500608	Queens of the Stone Age – Songs for the Deaf	$19.95
02500659	The Best of Bonnie Raitt	$24.95
02501268	Joe Satriani	$22.95
02501299	Joe Satriani – Crystal Planet	$24.95
02500306	Joe Satriani – Engines of Creation	$22.95
02501205	Joe Satriani – The Extremist	$22.95
02507029	Joe Satriani – Flying in a Blue Dream	$22.95
02501155	Joe Satriani – Professor Satchafunkilus and the Musterion of Rock	$24.95
02500544	Joe Satriani – Strange Beautiful Music	$22.95
02500920	Joe Satriani – Super Colossal	$22.95
02506959	Joe Satriani – Surfing with the Alien	$19.95
02500560	Joe Satriani Anthology	$24.99
02501255	Best of Joe Satriani	$19.95
02501238	Sepultura – Chaos A.D.	$19.95
02500188	Best of the Brian Setzer Orchestra	$19.95
02500985	Sex Pistols – Never Mind the Bollocks, Here's the Sex Pistols	$19.95
02501230	Soundgarden – Superunknown	$19.95
02500956	The Strokes – Is This It	$19.95
02501586	The Sword – Age of Winters	$19.99
02500799	Tenacious D	$19.95
02501035	Tenacious D – The Pick of Destiny	$19.95
02501263	Tesla – Time's Making Changes	$19.95
02501147	30 Easy Spanish Guitar Solos	$14.99
02500561	Learn Funk Guitar with Tower of Power's Jeff Tamelier	$19.95
02501440	Derek Trucks – Already Free	$24.95
02501007	Keith Urban – Love, Pain & The Whole Crazy Thing	$24.95
02500636	The White Stripes – Elephant	$19.95
02501095	The White Stripes – Icky Thump	$19.95
02500583	The White Stripes – White Blood Cells	$19.95
02501092	Wilco – Sky Blue Sky	$22.95
02500431	Best of Johnny Winter	$19.95
02500949	Wolfmother	$22.95
02500199	Best of Zakk Wylde	$22.99
02500700	Zakk Wylde – Legendary Licks	$19.95

Bass Transcriptions

02501108	Bass Virtuosos	$19.95
02500117	Black Sabbath – Riff by Riff Bass	$17.95
02506966	Guns N' Roses – Appetite for Destruction	$19.95
02501522	John Mayer Anthology for Bass, Vol. 1	$24.99
02500639	Metallica – St. Anger	$19.95
02500771	Best of Rancid for Bass	$17.95
02501120	Best of Tower of Power for Bass	$19.95
02500317	Victor Wooten Songbook	$22.95

Transcribed Scores

02500424	The Best of Metallica	$24.95
02500883	Mr. Big – Lean into It	$24.95

See your local music dealer or contact:

EXCLUSIVELY DISTRIBUTED BY

HAL•LEONARD CORPORATION

7777 W. BLUEMOUND RD. P.O. BOX 13819 MILWAUKEE, WI 53213

Prices, contents, and availability subject to change without notice.

0211